*The Middle East
and the
European Common Market*

The Middle East
and the
European Common Market

ROUHOLLAH K. RAMAZANI

Woodrow Wilson Department of Foreign Affairs
University of Virginia

THE UNIVERSITY PRESS OF VIRGINIA

Charlottesville

THE UNIVERSITY PRESS OF VIRGINIA

© 1964 by the Rector and Visitors of the
University of Virginia

First published 1964

Library of Congress Catalog Card Number: 64-13718
Printed in the United States of America
by Vail-Ballou Press, Inc.

To
Nesta, My Wife
For her sustaining encouragement and patience

Foreword

MORRIS R. COHEN, in his *Reason and Nature,* has pointed out that "a plurality of aspects is an essential trait of things in existence." The plurality of aspects implicit in the European Economic Community has not, on the whole, received the attention it deserves from analysts of international economic and political affairs, or for that matter from political leaders and administrators directly involved in the Community. The results of the present movement toward European economic union transcend the interests and affairs of the Community itself. The United States has a direct concern with the effects of economic union on its markets in the Community. But it is likewise concerned with the impact of European economic union on third areas as this impact may influence their relations with the United States, with the Communist bloc, and with the world at large. The pervasive and far-reaching influence of the creation of so massive a concentration of producing and consuming power as is instinct in the Common Market will undoubtedly have a profound effect not only upon the international economy but also upon international relations.

Professor Ramazani's study of *The Middle East and the European Common Market* is a brilliantly conceived and executed exploration in one of the more volatile of these third areas of the factors underlying the complex reactions of the Arab and non-Arab states of the Middle East to the Common Market. The essential facts concerning the reactions are clear: the Arab states, which have suffered least and probably stand to gain most in relations with the Community, are its severest critics; the non-Arab states, which have already encountered some economic dislocation in their relations with the Community and which may be confronted with further difficult and complicated adjustments in their trading and financial patterns as a consequence of the establishment of the Common Market, are favorably disposed toward it.

On the economic side, the book investigates in depth the significant facts concerning the impact which EEC policies are producing on several important sectors in the economies of the states of the Middle East. The policies of the Community as they affect the demand for petroleum, grain, vegetables and fruits, cotton, tobacco, and carpets and the policies of the states of the Middle East as they affect the competitive position of their exports in the Common Market are examined in detail. The problem of relations between the United Kingdom and the Common Market and the implications of these relations for Middle East trade with the Community are carefully appraised.

But the economic facts, which in a rational and well-ordered universe ought to be primary determinants of Middle East reaction to an essentially economic phenomenon, do not go very far toward explaining Middle East attitudes. Working from a wide variety of sources, Professor Ramazani examines the noneconomic factors in the Middle East reaction. These range from the hereditary enmity of Iran and Turkey toward Russia to Arab conflict with Israel and to Arab suspicion of Western "neocolonialism." The book also takes a good look at the association of African states in the Common Market, at "positive neutralism" among the Arabs, and at visions of an Arab Common Market as these factors condition Middle Eastern attitudes toward the Community.

Significantly, Professor Ramazani points out that the reaction of the Middle East toward the effects produced by the establishment of the Common Market is directed not primarily toward the European members of the Community, but rather toward the West. The attitude of the Arabs, therefore, is not a problem just for Brussels and Paris and Bonn and Rome, but for London, Washington, and Ottawa as well. And even more significantly, Professor Ramazani concludes that the unfriendly attitude of the Arab states toward the EEC or the West as a whole is a profound psychocultural problem which cannot be overcome by any degree of goodwill on the part of the West alone. The main responsibility for cooperation with the West lies not so much with Brussels or with Washington as with Baghdad, Cairo, and Damascus.

ROWLAND EGGER

Charlottesville, Virginia
March 6, 1964

Preface

THE COMMON MARKET is an evolving community which is yet to be fully established. At the present time it is in a transitional stage striving to forge a new community without meanwhile jeopardizing the interests of the smaller communities of the Six. Yet the European Economic Community (EEC) has officially been in existence since 1958, it has created unprecedented changes in the life of the peoples within its folds, it has produced global repercussions, and it has adopted significant policies ushering in dynamically new trends, which are, in the words of its architects, "irreversible."

This study is concerned with the impact of the Common Market on the Middle East and the reaction of that area to the Community. The overriding thesis is twofold: One is that the Common Market has adversely affected the export of a number of Middle East commodities, can produce further ill effects on such products, and may well adversely affect other exports of the area before and after the full establishment of the EEC. The selection of the Middle East export items under discussion here has been guided chiefly by two considerations—inclusion (1) of those commodities that have rather consistently been of particular significance in the exports of the Middle East to the Common Market countries and (2) of those export items for which the Common Market has already formulated policies or has adopted specific principles that should govern future policies.

The commodities thus selected belong to a total of nine Middle East countries. These are Egypt, Iran, Iraq, Israel, Kuwait, Lebanon, Saudi Arabia, Syria, and Turkey. Kuwait and Saudi Arabia, however, are included only in the discussion of the effect of the EEC on Middle East petroleum exports. The other seven countries are the principal exporters of nonpetroleum commodities to the Common Market, although Iran and Iraq are two of the major exporters of oil as well. Of these seven, the three non-Arab countries —Iran, Israel, and Turkey—have been the hardest hit by the development of the EEC. Although the exports of the Arab countries, by contrast, have not been so seriously affected, the Common Market has made itself felt on a number of their commodities. In the analysis of the actual or potential impact of the Common Market on Middle East exports attempt is made to consider not only the effects of the EEC as such, but also those of the countries which are already associated with or may later become members of the EEC. Since the association of Greece and a number of African states and the possibility of membership of Britain are of particular significance for the exports of the Middle East, the scope of the study is broadened to include these actual or potential effects also.

The other aspect of the main thesis of this study is that the relationship between the attitudes of the Middle East countries toward the EEC and the actual impact of the EEC on the Middle East exports is inverse in that the non-Arab countries have been seriously hurt but have sought accommodation with the EEC. The Arab countries, by contrast, have suffered less but have tended toward outright opposition to the Common Market. The non-Arab attempts at cooperation have taken varying forms as exemplified by Turkish application for association and Iran's decision to sign a limited agreement in order to protect its interests in regard to specific export items. The tone of the Arab opposition, within or without the Arab League, has been set primarily by Egypt, although more reasoned views on the EEC experiment have, at times, emanated from other Arab countries, notably Lebanon.

The paradoxical reaction of the Middle East to the Common Market is indicative of the significance of noneconomic factors in shaping the attitude of Middle East countries toward the EEC. Although the effects of the EEC on the exports of the non-Arab countries have been serious, these countries, as mentioned, have sought accommodation with the Common Market as the result of a number of historical, cultural, ideological, geographic, and, most important of all, political considerations. On the other hand, the Arab states of the Middle East have tended to oppose the EEC, principally because of the fears and suspicions with which they view the whole EEC experiment.

These fears are exerting far-reaching influences on the Arab attitude toward *the West as a whole*. For this reason the entire Atlantic Community should be concerned with the image that the EEC is producing in the strategic Middle East. The Common Market should not be allowed to become an additional instrument of alienation of the Arab Middle East in the Cold War. Rather it can and should be made an instrument for dispelling the current suspicions of the Arabs relative to the Atlantic Community as a whole, whether with a view to the immediate objective of supporting the independence of the Middle East countries against external aggression and internal subversion or toward the distant but worthy cause of creating an Atlantic–Middle East community which could hopefully become the nucleus of a new legal and political order for the world.

The organization of this study revolves around the twofold characteristic of its fundamental thesis. Part I treats the impact of the Common Market on Middle East exports. Chapters I–III each treat a specific sector of the Middle East exports. This approach by sectors, rather than by countries, has been preferred in the chapters dealing exclusively with the impact of the EEC on Middle East exports partly because it corresponds with the Common Market's actual approach to problems of policy. Although the EEC, as contrasted with the European Coal and Steel Community and Euratom, is an all-inclusive Community, it has adopted the sector approach in enacting rules and regulations and in formulating policies. Chapter IV treats those major exports of the Middle East which do not fall within any specific sector and yet must be discussed because the Common Market has affected them. Chapter V, again applying the sector approach, discusses Middle East exports to Great Britain because that country may possibly enter the Common Market and because British markets are of continuing significance for the Middle East.

Part II takes up the second portion of the main thesis. It is principally concerned with exposition of the factors shaping the attitudes of the Middle East countries toward the EEC. Since the harm to Middle East exports is treated in Part I, these chapters will allude to it only when it has a significant bearing on the policy of a given Middle East country. They will be devoted, in the main, to an examination of other significant factors underlying the reactions of the Middle East countries. The divergent characteristics of these reactions have made it analytically desirable to treat the reaction of non-Arab and Arab countries separately, in Chapters VI and VII. Chapter VIII attempts to synthesize the major points developed in the entire study and to indicate briefly the broader implications of the problems involved in the relations of the Middle East with the EEC. The general reader who may wish to concern himself only with the attitudes and policies of the Middle East countries toward the Common Market may, without too much difficulty, move on from the Preface to Part II.

In the preparation of this study a wide variety of sources in Middle Eastern as well as Western languages has been used. Most of these sources are cited in the footnotes. A number of these citations refer the reader to Appendix tables. These tables, all but two of which have been especially prepared for this work, are prefaced by a brief note pointing out their limitations as well as their rationale.

The author recognizes that this is by no means a definitive study. There is nothing definitive about the Middle East, or the Common Market. The chronic sociopolitical upheavals of the Middle East are too well known to require elaboration here. And, of course, the Common Market is still in the process of development. Because this is a preliminary study, it suffers from all the hazards accompanying the breaking of new ground. But I have accepted the risks in the hope that it may stimulate research and suggest themes for further exploration in this important field of Middle East relations with the West. As the reader proceeds, he may discern, for example, that such issues as the impact of the EEC on Middle East industrial development programs and on the direction of Middle East trade merit research. Or he may find, to cite more examples, that the problem of Soviet manipulation of Arab-African apprehensions regarding European unity, the problem of an Arab common market vis-à-vis the European Common Market or an Irano-Turko-Pakistani common market, or the effects of political shifts within Europe on the character of EEC policies toward the Middle East deserve exploration.

First and foremost I should like to acknowledge my deep indebtedness to Hon. Christian A. Herter, Special Representative for Trade Negotiations of the United States, for reading the manuscript and for his unreserved encouragement. I am also grateful to Professor Rowland Egger, my friend and chairman of the Departments of Foreign Affairs and Political Science at the University of Virginia, for writing the Foreword to this study.

I should also like to thank Mr. J. Mellick of the European Economic Community in Brussels, Mr. Leonard B. Tennyson and Mrs.

Ella Krucoff of the EEC Information Service in Washington, D.C., Mr. Mazen Nashashibi of Amman, Jordan, and Mr. Bernard Reich of Charlottesville, Virginia, for their assistance in my search for materials. Thanks should also be expressed to Messrs. Kenneth L. Murray and Stuart Learner of the United States Department of Agriculture and to Mr. Robert D. Sethian of the United States Department of Commerce for advice. Mr. Nathaniel Howell deserves special mention for his tireless assistance in the preparation of the tables. Heartfelt appreciation goes to Miss Ruth Ritchie, secretary in the Wilson Gee Institute for Research in the Social Sciences of the University of Virginia, for preparing the manuscript for publication.

R. K. R.

The University of Virginia
October 1963

Contents

PART II

*Middle East Attitudes and Policies toward the
European Common Market*

CONTENTS   xix

Appendix Tables, Index

Appendix Tables

xxi

PART I

*Impact of the European Common Market
on Middle East Exports*

I

Oil and Petroleum Products

THE European Economic Community (EEC), usually called the Common Market, became an entity on January 1, 1958, as the result of the signing of the Treaty of Rome between Belgium, the Federal Republic of Germany, France, Italy, Luxembourg, and the Netherlands on March 25, 1957. The establishment of the Common Market and the progressive implementation of the Treaty of Rome have had far-reaching effects on the exports of a large number of "third countries." Some countries such as Austria, Sweden, and Switzerland have applied for association with the Common Market under Article 238 of the Treaty of Rome. Others such as Argentina, Australia, New Zealand, Canada, and the United States have requested that their interests be reconciled with those of the Community by a liberal policy ensuring the maintenance of their markets and enabling them to benefit from the internal expansion of the Six. The United Kingdom has sought full membership in the EEC, and the Soviet Union has shown outright opposition to it.

The Middle East countries—Egypt, Iran, Iraq, Israel, Kuwait, Lebanon, Saudi Arabia, Syria, and Turkey—have not been untouched by the establishment of the European Common Market. Nor have they failed to develop attitudes and policies toward the

3

EEC. As traditional exporters of various products to the member countries of the Common Market, the Middle East countries have been affected variously by the Common Market and the progressive implementation of the Treaty of Rome. The exports of some Middle East countries such as Israel have been jeopardized, while those of others such as Iraq have suffered much less. First let us see how the Middle East's major export to the Market is faring.

As yet the Common Market has had no effect on Middle East oil and petroleum products, but the emerging energy policy of the EEC contains significant implications for the future export of these products. Although this policy is still being formulated, the basic interests and guiding principles are clearly discernible. These have been the subject of intensive study by the Executives of the European Coal and Steel Community (ECSC), Euratom, and the EEC. The oil policy of the EEC is inextricably bound up with its over-all energy policy, and both must therefore be considered in any discussion of the Market's implications for the export of Middle East oil and petroleum products.

These implications relate principally to the EEC's determination to substitute other sources of energy for oil as far as possible, to diversify its sources of energy, to adopt a common external tariff for petroleum products, and to obtain inexpensive supplies of oil. Only two of these measures pose serious challenges to the Middle East oil-exporting countries. One is diversification of sources of supply; the other is the Common Market's determination to secure cheap oil.

"PROGRESSIVITY OF SUBSTITUTES"

"Progressivity of substitutes" is one of the major principles that has been set forth by the European Parliament in its Resolution of February 20, 1962, and that guided the policy recommendations of the Inter-Executive Committee in its memorandum of June 25, 1962.[1] In order to show how the application of this principle will affect the oil-exporting countries of the Middle East, it is essential to inquire into the over-all problem of energy in Western Europe in general and in the Common Market countries in particular and simultaneously to relate this problem to the major sources of energy in relationship to one another.

Ever since 1948, when conditions in Europe began to assume postwar normality, there has been a steady increase in the demand for energy. In the area of the Organization for European Economic Cooperation (OEEC),[2] for example, consumption of primary energy increased from 526.6 million tons of coal equivalent in 1948 to 730.0 in 1955. Consumption of crude petroleum increased from 53.9 million tons of coal equivalent in 1948 to 126.0 in 1955. Had Europe's own sources of energy been sufficient to meet this rise in energy consumption, there would have been no urgent problem. But this has not been the case. In 1955, for example, the entire OEEC area produced 584 million tons of coal equivalent of energy while its consumption amounted to 730 million. This gap between the consumption and the production of energy has been attributed to the rapidly increasing consumption of oil and the relative poverty of Western Europe's oil fields and to the slow rise in coal production as compared with the more rapid rise in primary

---

[1] This memorandum was drawn up by the Inter-Executive Committee established by the High Authority of ECSC and the Commissions of the EEC and Euratom. Published in 1962 under the title *Memorandum on Energy Policy*, it was prepared in accordance with the instructions of the ministers of the six countries and represented the joint proposals of the Executives of the European Communities for the definition of an energy policy.

[2] The OEEC was transformed into the Organization for Economic Cooperation and Development in December, 1960. The new organization was brought about in the main as a result of the United States' determination to create a transatlantic framework within which the EEC and the European Free Trade Area (EFTA) in particular could cooperate. The eighteen-member OEEC is now composed of twenty members, with the addition of the United States and Canada, and is designated as OECD.

energy consumption.[3] In turn, the rapid increase in the consumption of oil is attributed to its growing use in transport of all kinds, to the advantages of oil over other fuels for certain purposes, and to the rise of coal prices.[4]

In broad terms, what has just been said in regard to the gap between energy consumption and production in the OEEC countries also holds true for the Common Market. Obviously, the consumption as well as the production figures become smaller in regard to the Common Market, in part for the reason that there are only six countries in the Market as contrasted with eighteen in the OEEC. For example, the consumption of primary energy in the OEEC area amounted to nearly 6 million tons of coal equivalent in 1950 while that of the Common Market area was nearly 3 million. But this figure is based upon the consumption of Germany, Belgium, France, Italy, Luxembourg, and the Netherlands before they decided to lay the foundations of the Common Market.[5] One of the fundamental goals of the Common Market is economic development, and availability of energy is a necessity for all development. It is foreseen that between 1960 and 1975 the European Community's energy requirements will rise from 460 million to 850 million tons of coal equivalent. This estimate is based upon the outlook for rapid growth in the Community's economy (4.6 per cent per annum for the national product) which should increase total energy requirements to about 4 per cent per annum.

Can the Common Market meet this energy problem from its own resources? Coal has traditionally been one of the most important sources of energy in the Market area, but in recent years its significance has diminished. For example, in 1950, 70 per cent of the energy requirements were met with coal, but by 1960 the per-

---

[3] OEEC, *Europe's Growing Needs of Energy: How Can They Be Met?* (Paris, 1956), p. 24.

[4] *Ibid.*, p. 31.

[5] EEC, *The European Community's Long-Term Energy Prospects* (Brussels, 1963), p. 2.

centage was only 52 per cent. The decline of coal has been caused partly by technological factors and partly by difficulty in adjusting to the lower prices of competing sources of energy.[6] Furthermore, this decline will probably continue in the future. It would be

unrealistic to envisage a total coal production rising above the present level. On the contrary, coal production is more likely to be progressively scaled down by the closure of the least economic pits. . . . The other traditional internal sources of energy—with the possible exception of natural gas—are not such as could be developed to any significant extent in comparison with the rapid expansion of energy requirements. The increase in consumption will therefore be largely in that of oil and possibly of American coal, pending the juncture at which nuclear energy can begin to play a growing role, from about 1970.[7]

From this it is evident that the Common Market countries realize that coal as a source of energy will not be able to keep up with the swift expansion of their energy consumption and that at least until 1970 oil will be increasingly in demand. The Middle East has traditionally supplied over 80 per cent of Europe's oil requirements and, barring unpredictable circumstances, there is every reason to believe that the flow of Middle East oil to the Common Market will continue and increase. But this statement will have to be read in light of the discussions that follow.

While the Common Market countries are not optimistic about the prospects of coal, they are looking forward to the increasing possibilities of utilization of nuclear energy. A common market for nuclear products, plant, and personnel has already been established, the Second Five-Year research program on nuclear energy is in effect, and the Common Market is working with the ECSC and Euratom with a view to increasing the use of nuclear power as a source of energy. In discussing this question, however, it is necessary to distinguish between two periods. From all available evidence

[6] *Memo. on Energy Policy*, p. 17.   [7] *Ibid.*, p. 11.

it is clear that nuclear energy will not be a competitive source before 1970. This is true in spite of the fact that nuclear energy has already been utilized to produce electric power in a number of countries. But from 1970 on, there is every reason to believe that large power stations will be in a competitive position. In 1970 the contribution of nuclear electricity to the Community's energy supply will be 8 million tons of coal equivalent, but in 1975 it will be between 24 and 40 million, or 3 to 5 per cent of total supplies.[8] By 1975 it is also anticipated that petroleum will supply about 52 per cent of the total energy requirements as compared with 27 per cent in 1960. It is also predicted that by 1975 about 50 per cent of the total energy will be supplied from imports of petroleum as compared with 23 per cent in 1960.[9]

What the exact implications of all this will be for Middle East oil exports after 1975 cannot be fully determined inasmuch as a great many variables are involved. For example, it may be asked what the price of Middle East oil will be by that time, how cheaply the Community will be able to produce atomic energy, whether it will be possible to utilize nuclear power for purposes other than the production of electric current, and whether it will be possible to utilize such power in transportation, which is now so extensively dependent on oil. The number of such questions may easily be enlarged, but it must now be clear that it would be impossible to predict with any significant degree of accuracy how the development of nuclear energy after 1975 will affect the exports of Middle East oil to the Common Market. Before 1975 there will be no serious cause for concern on the part of the oil-exporting countries of the Middle East about the utilization of nuclear energy by the Common Market unless there is a significant break-through in this respect. On the other hand, the prospects for atomic power as a source of

[8] *Bulletin of the European Economic Community*, February, 1963, p. 29.
[9] *Ibid.*

energy after 1975 seem to be promising—a probability of which the Middle East exporters of oil may well take note in formulating their future oil policy. In the meantime Europe will undoubtedly continue to import substantial quantities of Middle East crude oil, partly because the proven reserves and the rate of production in the area rank so high in comparison with the rest of the world.

It must be understood that, unlike coal and some minerals, estimates of recoverable oil involve uncertainties. Figures on "proven reserves" are available, although discrepancies in estimates can be observed. With this note of caution in mind, let us examine the published data for the year 1960. These show that the United States, Venezuela, and the Middle East are the three major sites of oil reserves. In that year the "proven reserves" of these areas constituted 88 per cent of the world reserves. However, the United States' share was 13.7 per cent and Venezuela's 7.2 per cent, while the Middle East's share was 67.2 per cent. A different source puts the Middle East percentage at the slightly lower level of 60.9. Four major oil-producing countries account for the bulk of this figure. Kuwait's reserves at 20 per cent lead those of Saudi Arabia at 16.8, Iran's at 11.3, and Iraq's at 8.6. Oil exploration and drilling are at present under way, and the prospects of strikes in various parts of the area will undoubtedly cause an upward revision in these estimates.[10]

As a large-scale producer, the Middle East is a relative newcomer to the world oil industry. However, its average rate of expansion in the postwar decade has been much higher than that for the world, justifying Dr. De Golyer's celebrated observation in 1944 that "the center of gravity of world oil production is shifting from the Gulf-Caribbean area to the Middle East and is likely to continue to shift until it is firmly established in that area." In the 1958–61 period the production of crude oil increased 31 per cent; this compared favorably with world production during the same period at 23 per

[10] See Table 1.

cent. The four major oil-producing countries have maintained their share of the total oil output of the Middle East at approximately 92 per cent.

THE TARIFF POLICY

Another means by which the Common Market could affect the exports of Middle East oil is its tariff policy. Although the oil policy has yet to be formulated fully in conjunction with the over-all energy policy of the European Community, its general framework is clearly visible at the present time. Before discussing this, however, it is essential to examine briefly the role of Western Europe in Middle East oil exports.

The overwhelming dependence of Middle Eastern oil-producing countries on the Western market (the markets in Western Europe and in the Americas) is shown by oil export figures for 1960. During this year their total exports to the West amounted to over 160 million tons, while their total exports to the rest of the world were slightly over 56 million tons.

Western Europe has long been the most important customer of Middle Eastern crude oil. In 1958 the Middle East exported a total of over 170 million tons of crude oil; Western Europe received 109 million tons. In 1959 Western Europe imported almost 120 million tons of the Middle East's total exports of about 189 million tons. This steady increase reached a new peak in 1961, when Western Europe received over 140 million tons of the Middle East's total of over 237 million.[11]

How would the Common Market tariff policy affect these oil exports? The Treaty of Rome committed its signatories to a number of short-run objectives for the achievement of which a common market is to be established gradually. These objectives include promotion of harmonious development of economic activities through-

[11] See Table 3.

out the Community, continuous and balanced expansion of the economy, increased stability, accelerated raising of standards of living, and closer relations between the member states.[12] One of the major ways by which the Common Market is to secure these objectives is the establishment of a common customs tariff and a common commercial policy toward third countries. Creation of a common customs tariff is to be effected gradually rather than overnight. The Treaty of Rome provides a timetable consisting of three major stages of alignment of national tariffs, with the third stage ending on December 31, 1969. By that time the national tariffs of the six member states will have been fully aligned on the customs tariff of the Common Market. In other words, by the end of the third stage the existing tariff systems of the six countries will have been replaced by a single external tariff vis-à-vis imports from the rest of the world, including the Middle East.

Thus the Market's common external tariff on oil imports from the Middle East must be treated in two parts—before and after 1970. The first period involves the question whether the national tariffs within the framework of the Market are being aligned and, if so, whether they are affecting the importation of oil from the Middle East. The overriding question of the second period is what the nature of the single external tariff will be after 1970.

As a result of the decisions of the Council of Ministers of the Common Market on May 12, 1960, and May 15, 1962, the timetable of the Treaty of Rome has been speeded up, and the first alignment of national tariffs took place at the beginning of 1961. This alignment produced no new tariff barrier on oil. It was stated in June, 1962, that "most imports of crude oil and petroleum products from third countries outside the Eastern bloc are already free of restrictions."[13] So far as Middle East oil is concerned, the flow

---

[12] *Treaty Establishing the European Economic Community and Connected Documents* (n.p., n.d.), Art. 2.

[13] *Memo. on Energy Policy*, p. 26.

to the Common Market continued unimpeded after the first alignment. Iran, Iraq, Saudi Arabia, and Kuwait exported crude oil to
the Common Market in 1961 worth $297,624,000, $412,342,000,
$261,318,000, and $436,970,000, respectively. In the same order
these countries exported petroleum products to the Common Market worth $4,183,000, $7,177,000, $2,443,000, and $6,402,000.[14]

In considering post-1970 tariff policy, a distinction must be made
between crude oil and petroleum products. List F attached to the
Treaty of Rome provided that there be no duties on crude oil after
1970. This has been fully endorsed by the Executives of the Common Market. In their Memorandum of June 25, 1962, they recommended "unrestricted importation of crude oil. . . ." So far as
petroleum products are concerned, List G of the Treaty will be
applicable. This list, however, does not specify what the single
external tariff on petroleum products should be. Rather it leaves
the level of the tariff to be decided through negotiations among
the six member countries. The Executive group in the memorandum just mentioned suggested that duties on imports of petroleum
products should be low. In any event, this should present no serious difficulty for the Middle East as the figures on crude oil and
petroleum products exported to the Common Market clearly show
that petroleum products constitute only a small percentage of the
total volume of exports to the EEC. The reason for the small volume is that major refinery products of the Middle East constitute
a small percentage of the world total. In 1960, for example, the
Middle East accounted for only 7.8 per cent of the world total.
So far as the Common Market tariff is concerned, Middle East oil-
exporting countries will have little reason to worry about their exports of crude oil even after 1970, and the degree to which their
petroleum products will be adversely affected will depend upon the
level of the common external tariff on these products, and that is
yet to be determined.

[14] See Tables 4–7.

DIVERSIFICATION OF SOURCES OF SUPPLY

One of the major principles set forth by the European Parliament in its resolution mentioned previously is "security of supply." The political disturbances that have affected Middle East oil exports to Western Europe in the past must have had a significant bearing on the enunciation of this principle. The Suez crisis is a major case in point. But it is not the only one. The chronic political instability of the Middle East is an important factor in the policy calculations of the Common Market countries, which are greatly dependent on the availability of Middle East oil for acceleration of economic growth and betterment of the standards of living.

Security of supply, according to the recommendations of the Common Market Executives, can be achieved in part through diversification of the sources of supply. On this basis it has been suggested that the European Community should avoid complete dependence on outside supplies but should ensure that its energy requirements are partly covered by intra-Community resources. So far as oil is concerned, however, the resources of the Common Market countries are meager, although it is hoped that intensive prospecting within Europe will lead to the opening up of fairly substantial reserves of oil. Nevertheless, the fact remains that the Community's own production of oil in 1960 supplied only 4 per cent of the total, and this will decrease to a mere 2 per cent by 1975.[15]

Because of the importance of diversification of sources of supply it has been suggested that sources other than those of the Middle East must be considered, in spite of the fact that imports from other places will undoubtedly be more expensive.[16] For the immediate

[15] See EEC, *The European Community's Long-Term Energy Prospects*, p. 6, table.

[16] *Memo. on Energy Policy*, pp. 15–16.

future a most attractive non-Middle Eastern source is the Sahara.

The Sahara has been the scene of intensive exploration since 1953, and it is now known to contain petroleum and natural gas deposits of potentially great importance. It was stated in 1959 that the discoveries in the Sahara may mean a flow of 50 million tons by 1965 and 100 million tons by 1975. Natural gas, of even greater interest to industry as a source of energy, may be flowing from the Sahara in amounts around 30 million tons by 1965 and 60 million tons by 1975.[17] If activities continue as planned, it is estimated that by the end of 1960 about 8 million tons a year of Saharan oil would reach the Mediterranean coast, rising perhaps to 25 to 30 million tons a year by the mid-1960's. This would compete with Middle East supplies to Europe.[18]

Should French insistence on obtaining special preference for Algerian oil in the Common Market succeed, Middle East oil may find itself, about 1965, at least partially shut out from the countries in the Common Market.[19] It may be added also that Middle East oil may face even tougher competition by 1975 if, in addition to Algerian oil, the huge increase in natural gas in the Common Market itself as well as in Algeria reaches the level now predicted. Algerian natural gas is to rise to 60 million tons by 1975, and the Common Market's own natural gas has quadrupled since 1958 and is expected to amount to about 40 million tons by 1975.[20]

It should be realized, however, that optimism on the part of the Common Market countries of finding non-Middle East supply sources must be tempered by several considerations. First, Sahara oil has a high proportion of light products, and this makes it less suit-

[17] *Bulletin from the European Community*, June–July, 1959, p. 6.

[18] Economist Intelligence Unit Limited and the Cartographic Department of the Clarendon Press, *Oxford Regional Economic Atlas: The Middle East and North Africa* (Oxford, 1960), p. 94.

[19] Wayne A. Leeman, *The Price of Middle East Oil: An Essay in Political Economy* (Ithaca, 1962), pp. 45–46.

[20] *Bull. from Eur. Com.*, June–July, 1959, p. 6.

able as a fuel oil for European consumption.[21] Second, the assumption that Algeria will be a more reliable source for oil is at best questionable considering the revolutionary and nationalistic fervor of the Arab world, which has infected Algeria.

Another non-Middle Eastern source of supply which must be considered is the Soviet. As a result of a concentrated drive Western Europe in recent years has been increasingly supplied with Soviet oil. It was reported in 1962 that Western Europe was meeting 9 per cent of its demand by imports of Russian oil, imports which will probably reach 11 per cent by 1965. West Germany and Italy in particular have been good customers. In 1960, for example, Italy was the largest customer of the Soviet Union, taking nearly 4 million tons of crude oil. Italy's purchases of Russian oil have taken place "at the expense of oil from the Middle East" and have apparently been of "serious concern to the Arab countries." [22] It is important to note, however, that the Common Market Executives have recommended that a Community quota system in respect to imports from countries of the Eastern bloc should be established.[23]

---

[21] *Ibid.*

[22] Leon M. Herman, "The Soviet Oil Offensive," *The Reporter*, June 21, 1962, pp. 26–28. The Treaty of Rome provides for gradual harmonization of commerical policies of the EEC countries. One of the special problems in this respect is the importation of petroleum from the Soviet Union. The EEC report in referring to this problem stated that "in 1961 they [oil imports from the Soviet Union] amounted to 10.3 million metric tons for the Community as a whole and represented 7.2% of available resources. In 1960 the Member States had imported 8.1 million tons—6.5% of available resources. At present such imports are subject to quotas in five countries while remaining free of such restrictions in the sixth and this leaves a loophole for the diversion of trade, which, if it should develop, could lead to the application of safeguard measures and the isolation of the markets. The European Commission has sought to remedy this state of affairs, with due regard to the legitimate interests of the various countries. A first result was obtained in the framework of the general agreement reached in the Council on 25 July 1961. This provided for consultation prior to the conclusion of any trade agreement with non-member countries" (EEC Commission, *Fifth General Report on the Activities of the Community* [1 May 1961—30 April 1962], [n.p., 1962], p. 131).

[23] *Memo. on Energy Policy*, p. 17.

"CHEAPNESS OF SUPPLY"

Another principle that is to guide the Common Market's oil policy is "cheapness of supply." It is clear that the Common Market countries are determined to acquire cheap oil. The Energy Committee of the European Parliament seemed to be more concerned with the price of oil than with security of supply when it remarked that "there is every prospect that Europe will not lack for energy in the future—but at what price?" The Common Market countries are aware that the problem of prices may assume added significance in the future, but they are hopeful that the Community's negotiating position vis-à-vis the producer countries will be strengthened as a result of its increasing purchases of crude oil. Such optimism, however, must be restrained by the seriousness with which the oil-exporting countries of the Middle East view the whole price problem. As this problem may well prove to be a most important issue between the Middle East producers and the Common Market consumers in the years to come, it must now be considered. But first the opposition of the Middle East exporters to price reductions must be understood in light of the indirect as well as direct benefits that they derive from oil operations.

Benefits from oil operations in the Middle East accrue to the countries in various ways. The most obvious way is, of course, direct payments. The amount of the payments is determined by the terms of the concessions, the volume of crude output, and the prices of crude oil. Ever since the early 1950's the renegotiated terms of the concessions have increased the oil income of the Middle Eastern countries. In 1960, for example, direct payments amounted to $1,374,000,000. The four major oil-producing countries of the area received the bulk of this income. Kuwait received $409,000,000, Saudi Arabia $332,000,000, Iran $285,000,000, and Iraq $267,-000. Payments are also made to some of the non-oil-producing countries of the Middle East in the form of oil transit fees. Payments are made by the Trans-Arabian Pipeline Company to Jordan, Lebanon, and Syria for carrying Saudi Arabian oil through pipelines to Sidon. Lebanon and Syria receive oil transit fees also from the Iraq Petroleum Company for carrying Iraqi oil through its pipelines to Tripoli and Banias. Egypt derives revenues from oil transport through the Suez Canal. In 1961 Lebanon earned $4,100,000, Syria $25,600,000, and Egypt $102,000,000. The contribution of the oil industry to the economies of the Middle East "goes beyond the direct payments received by the Governments of the area in the form of royalties, taxes and transit dues. The 1948–58 operating and capital expenditures of the petroleum companies in the Middle East exceeded $3,855 million, 42 per cent of which represented wages and salaries, payments to local contractors and purchases of local contractors and purchases of local supplies." [24]

These indirect as well as direct benefits have been made possible by enormous capital expenditures by Western private and public interests. The gross investment representing carrying values in property, plant, and equipment amounted (before deduction of retirements) to a billion dollars in 1946 but rose to over $4,000,000,000 in 1960. More than $3,000,000,000 of this amount represented capital expenditures on production, pipelines, refineries, and marketing. Further increases in investment are to be expected as the exploration and drilling activities are augmented and the existing refineries are expanded. Exploration and drilling activities are pushed not only in areas such as Muscat and Oman, where oil in commercial quantities has yet to be found, but also in countries such as Iran and Iraq, which are already two of the largest oil producers of the Middle East. In Iran far more vigorous exploration and drilling activities are in evidence than in Iraq. Iran-Italian Petroleum Company's offshore well No. 1 has produced 16,000 bar-

[24] UN, *Economic Developments in the Middle East, 1959–1961* (New York, 1962), p. 58.

rels a day, and Iran–Pan American Oil Company (IPAC) after extensive drilling is producing 35,000 barrels a day from its well Darius No. 1.

The benefits accruing to the oil-producing countries are not confined to the items enumerated above. In the absence of any systematic study of the socioeconomic impact of the oil industry on these countries a few more examples may be given.[25] This impact is also evident in recruitment practices, in training programs, in health services of both a curative as well as a preventive nature, in social insurance, in housing, in education, and even in recreation and shopping facilities. In addition, three of the major oil-producing countries of the Middle East have earmarked substantial portions of their revenues for development purposes. The pioneering step in this respect was taken by Iran as early as 1949 in conjunction with its first Seven-Year Plan, followed by Iraq in 1951, and finally by Kuwait. In Iran, for example, in the 1954–58 period a total of 25,137,000,000 rials was spent by the Plan Organization on development in agriculture and irrigation, in industry and mining, in transport and communications, and in the social sector. The total revenues on which the Plan Organization drew during the same period amounted to 20,432,000,000 rials. Of this amount 18,949,-000,000 rials represented receipts from petroleum revenues.[26] Both Iran and Iraq are determined to continue to devote large amounts of their oil revenues to the future development of their economies. Iran envisages spending 147,300,000,000 rials from oil revenues through its Third Development Plan during the period from 1962 to 1978. Iraq plans to spend 315,800,000 dinars of its oil income on development projects in the course of the 1961–65 period.[27]

[25] A valuable study was made by the International Labour Organization on Iran in 1950. Although somewhat dated at the present time, it contains reliable information on the socioeconomic impact of the oil industry on Iran (ILO Office, *Labor Conditions in the Oil Industry in Iran* [Geneva, 1950]).

[26] Information derived from UN, *Economic Developments in the Middle East, 1956–1957* (New York, 1958), p. 29, table.

[27] UN, *Economic Developments M.E., 1959–1961*, pp. 172–73.

From what has been said it is clear that the present and future economic development of the Middle East countries, particularly the oil-exporting countries, is closely linked with their revenues from oil. The prices for crude oil include royalties paid to the governments of the producer countries. These prices work out at about $5.00 a ton out of a posted price of about $12.50.[28] The recent reduction in prices has already caused considerable controversy involving both the governments and the oil companies. In fact, this problem has caused the Middle East producers to organize their efforts in the form of two different groupings.

The opposition of the oil-exporting countries to reductions in prices was first voiced in 1959, when they experienced losses in their expected revenues as a result of such reductions. The second reduction in the posted prices of crude oil in August, 1960, brought Iran, Iraq, Kuwait, and Saudi Arabia (and Venezuela from outside the Middle East) together in a meeting in Baghdad the next month. This meeting set the foundation for the Organization of Petroleum Exporting Countries (OPEC) with its headquarters in Geneva. Since then several meetings have been held, such as the ones held in Caracas and Tehran. The overriding concern of the Organization at all these meetings has been prices. In the Caracas meeting of January, 1961, it was clearly stated that the member countries had as their primary objective the restoration of crude oil prices to the pre-August, 1960, level.[29]

Although the Arab Petroleum Congress (APC) has been primarily concerned with the desire of the various countries to participate more fully in the activities of the oil industry, it also has opposed price reductions for oil products as well as for crude oil and has demanded that the oil companies not resort to price cutting without the consent of the Arab oil-producing countries. APC was organized under the auspices of the Arab League and has held sev-

[28] For a detailed examination of this problem, see Leeman, *op. cit.*
[29] UN, *Economic Developments M.E.*, 1959–1961, pp. 61–62.

eral meetings at which basically similar resolutions were passed incorporating Arab aspirations in regard to greater participation in the affairs of the oil industry, better technical and vocational training for Arabs, improvement of the terms of the existing oil concessions, and the like.[30]

The dependence of the Common Market countries on Middle East oil and, in turn, the need of the oil-producing and oil-transporting countries of the Middle East for revenues from the sale of oil to the Common Market provide both parties with strong bargaining positions. In opposing the association of Israel with the EEC the Arab countries threatened the Common Market by alluding to their oil. But obviously the denial of their oil to the Common Market would hurt their economies. So far this mutual dependence has been utilized for political or economic pressures. But it could also be used for forging a greater community of interests between the Common Market and the Middle East.

[30] *Ibid.*, pp. 62–64.

II

The Grain Sector

B ARLEY, wheat, and rice are the principal Middle East grain exports that have been affected by the Common Market. So far the effects have not been extensive, because the EEC's need for hard wheat has persisted and the levies on rice have not yet been conclusively determined. However, future effects on these commodities may be significant because of the probability of higher levies, because of developments within the EEC, and because of the association of African states with the Common Market.

THE NONPETROLEUM EXPORTS OF THE MIDDLE EAST
TO THE COMMON MARKET

Of the four major oil-exporting countries, Iran and Iraq are also major exporters of nonpetroleum products. In 1960, for example, Iran's agricultural products accounted for about 50 per cent of the value of its total exports, and Iraq's agricultural products (including dates) accounted for 73 per cent of its total exports.[1] With regard to the Common Market countries oil has consistently accounted for more than half of the value of the total exports of these

[1] UN, *Economic Developments in the Middle East, 1959–1961* (New York, 1962), p. 84.

countries.[2] But the value of nonpetroleum exports has been by no means insignificant. In 1956, for example, Iran's nonpetroleum exports to the Common Market countries amounted to nearly $95,000,000 and Iraq's was nearly $18,000,000.[3]

Iran and Iraq are not the only major exporters of nonpetroleum products to the Common Market countries. Turkey, Syria, Egypt, Lebanon, and Israel export substantially to Market countries. A comparison of the value of the exports of these countries to the Common Market reveals that Turkey has consistently ranked as the most important exporter of nonpetroleum products. In spite of the temporary decline of its exports to Common Market countries in 1956–57, due to increased trade with the Soviet Union and the Soviet bloc, Egypt also ranks high in terms of the value of its exports to the Common Market. Egypt's exports increased from $78,385,000 in 1957 to $83,309,000 in 1961. Turkey's exports in the same period, however, increased from $118,205,000 to $152,-881,000.

Syria should also be included among the leading exporters of nonpetroleum products to the Common Market. Its exports of $52,-892,000 in 1957 increased to $127,895,000 in 1961. It should be noted, however, that over $10,000,000 of the 1961 figure was for oil exports. Nevertheless, Syria is not a major oil-exporting country and its exports for nonpetroleum products in 1961 amounted to over $100,000,000. Lebanon and Israel are also important exporters of nonpetroleum products to the Common Market. In 1961, for example, Israel exported $127,895,000 and Lebanon exported $57,-215,000.

Thus the establishment of the Common Market is of concern to the countries of the Middle East with respect to products other than oil. This is particularly true because of the fact that most of the nonpetroleum exports of the Middle East to the Common Market consist of agricultural products, and the Common Market has

---

[2] Cf. Tables 3, 9, and 10.   [3] See Tables 16 and 17.

already taken momentous steps to regulate in detail such imports.

The Treaty of Rome in Articles 38–47 inclusive sets forth the general principles that should govern the extension of the Common Market to agriculture and trade in agricultural products. Article 38(4) of the Treaty expressly provides that "the functioning and development of the Common Market in respect of agricultural products shall be accompanied by the establishment of a common agricultural policy among the Member States." In compliance with the mandate of this article the Common Market has begun to formulate a complete agricultural policy. As contrasted with the Market's evolving oil policy, the agricultural policy is crystallized in the sense that the Community has already decided not only on the basic features of the common agricultural policy but also on the actual regulations of certain specific sectors in the agricultural field.

On January 14, 1962, the Council of Ministers of the European Economic Community ended a long session of twenty-three days during which it approved the essentials of the first common agricultural policy for Europe. "There are no other examples," declared Professor Walter Hallstein, President of the EEC Commission, "of such meetings of Europe's statesmen and officials of the highest rank lasting so long, working so intensively, and devoted so wholeheartedly to the cause of European progress. It is a conclusive proof of the reality of our Community and of its ability to take political decisions of the first order." This agreement was described by Rolf Lahr, Undersecretary of State in the German Ministry of Foreign Affairs, as a "new Rome Treaty."

The broad principles of the common agricultural policy are as follows:

1) To balance supply and demand both within the Community and in its external trade, by action on supply and demand;

2) To provide a fair income to farmers by structural and regional improvements;

3) To stabilize agricultural markets by protecting them from speculative price fluctuations without cutting them off from the influence of long-term movements in the world markets;

4) To ensure a fair deal to consumers by enabling the processing industries and trade to find external outlets at reasonable and competitive prices, and by preventing prices from being fixed on the basis of marginal production costs.[4]

At present the agricultural policy of the Common Market includes detailed regulations in regard to four major sectors. These regulations concern grain, pigmeat, eggs and poultry, and fruit and vegetables. The grain and fruit and vegetables sectors are of particular significance to Middle Eastern exporters. The remainder of this chapter will treat the grain sector.

BARLEY AND WHEAT

Regulation No. 19 pertains to the grain sector, although the term used is "cereals." Cereals are described therein in terms of processed and nonprocessed products.[5] Only the latter category is of particular importance to the Middle East. This category includes wheat and maslin, rye, barley, oats, maize, buckwheat, millet, canary seed, "grain," and sorghum. Most Middle East countries produce a number of these commodities, but wheat and barley figure significantly in their exports to Market countries. The two leading exporters of wheat and barley are Syria and Iraq. In 1956, for example, Syria exported over $10,000,000 worth of barley to the Common Market countries and Iraq exported nearly $10,000,000. In that same year Syria's wheat exports to the Common Market countries amounted to more than $3,000,000; Iraq's were negligible. Viewed over a number of years, Syria seems to rank as the most

[4] Official Spokesman of the Community, EEC, *A Farm Policy for Europe* (Brussels, 1962), pp. 5–6.

[5] See EEC Commission, *Regulations and Decisions in the Field of Agriculture Adopted by the Council on 14 January 1962*, Art. 1.

important exporter of wheat to the Common Market and Iraq as the most important exporter of barley.[6]

Discussion of the Common Market's agricultural policy in relation to exports of Iraqi barley and Syrian wheat must take account of two distinct periods of time. The first period began on July 1, 1962, and will end on December 31, 1969. During these seven and a half years all wheat and barley, as well as other grains, imported into Market countries are subject to the levy system put into force as a result of the decisions of the Council of Ministers. From 1970 on, when the existing national levy systems will be completely abolished, all wheat and barley exports to the Common Market from the outside world including the Middle East will be subjected to a single external levy system.

The existing levy systems are twofold in the sense that they are calculated in one way for intra-Community trade and in another way for imports from the outside world. The internal levy system has superseded the previous wide variety of tariffs, quotas, and minimum prices in operation within the boundaries of the six member countries. The new levy system is inextricably linked to a new price system. The price system consists of target prices for various grains, intervention prices, and threshold prices. Generally speaking, the target price is announced by each Common Market country for each product, taking into account the producer price level desired. The intervention (or support) price is also determined by each country for individual products. The purpose of the intervention price is "to afford producers a guarantee that the market price will be constantly maintained at a level as close as possible to the target price."[7] The intervention price, however, should be equal to the target price, less a fixed percentage within a range between 5 and 10 per cent. The threshold price derives from the target price minus the freight and marketing costs.

[6] Cf. Tables 13 and 17.
[7] See preamble of Regulation No. 19 in EEC, *Regulations*.

The levy system during the transition period may be studied from two different and related angles. One inquires whether the new system has, in the last analysis, created higher duties than before on imports of wheat and barley into Market countries. The other inquires whether the intra-Community levy has created conditions unfavorable to the importation of these products from the outside world, including the Middle East.

A general comparison of the existing levy system with previous restrictions and duties would require analysis of the situation in each of the six Common Market countries. This is not necessary for our purposes. Since Syria's wheat and Iraq's barley have been exported chiefly to the Republic of West Germany, a brief description of the present German levy system under the common agricultural policy as compared with its past system, which incidentally was also a variable levy system, will suffice. It must be realized, however, that the levy system changes constantly, and therefore figures for a specific date do not necessarily hold true for other dates. But it may be helpful to point out in general terms how the present levy system compares with the past one.

The levy on imports of wheat and barley into Germany or any other Common Market country is calculated on the basis of the threshold price, which, of course, is not the same in all the Common Market countries. Nor is it the same for both wheat and barley in a given country. The variable import levy is the threshold price minus the most favorable price on the world market. The application of this general formula to Germany with its particular target prices for barley and wheat reveals that the new levy on wheat on August 1, 1962, amounted to $61.25 a ton, whereas the previous levy was only $45.00. The levy on barley on the same date was $49.40, whereas the previous levy was only $36.00 a ton.[8]

The impact of intra-Community trade on exports of Middle East

___

[8] U.S. Department of Agriculture, *Foreign Agricultural Circular*, prepared by Kenneth L. Murray (Washington, August, 1962), p. 6.

wheat and barley during the transition period may be readily seen in the twofold character of the new levy system and the philosophy underlying it. From the general principles of the Treaty of Rome in regard to agriculture and trade in agricultural products to the detailed regulations for the gradual establishment of a common market in cereals, it is unmistakably clear that the member states are to be favored. This is best shown in the relationship of the internal levy system and the external levy. Outside suppliers get world prices while member-country exporters get their own internal prices. Since EEC internal prices are far above world prices, the levy on imports from third countries is much larger than that collected on imports from member countries.[9]

This favoring of intra-Community trade has significant implications for third countries which export commodities produced in the Common Market area. Wheat and barley are increasingly produced in this area and are favored over imports of these cereals from the Middle East. The problem is not, however, the creation of the Common Market inasmuch as the increasing production of wheat and barley antedates Market years. Prewar production of wheat in the present EEC countries averaged about 16 per cent, but it rose to a maximum of over 38 per cent in 1954–59. For barley the increase was from about 18 per cent to about 37 per cent. This expanding production has been generally attributed to mechanization, to the use of larger amounts of chemical fertilizers, to greater use of selected seeds and plants, and to the introduction of new and more productive varieties of seeds and plants.[10] But in spite of the fact that increasing production in the EEC countries is traceable to the period before the creation of the Common Market, there is no denying the equally important

[9] *Ibid.,* p. 3.
[10] EEC Commission, *Proposals for the Working Out and Putting into Effect of the Common Agricultural Policy in Application of Article 43 of the Treaty Establishing the European Economic Community* (Brussels, 1960; VI/COM [60]105), pp. 1–7.

fact that the lowering of trade barriers as a result of the Common Market has increased intra-Community trade unprecedentedly. In 1959 it was reported that the value of trade between the six countries, as compared with the corresponding periods of 1958, rose by 16 per cent in the second quarter, 22 per cent in the third, and 29 per cent in the fourth quarter. For the whole year the average increase was 19 per cent over 1958 and 15 per cent over 1957.[11] In 1961 intra-Community trade in terms of value totaled nearly $12,000,000,000. This was 16 per cent higher than the total for 1960. This rate of progress was still very satisfactory to the Common Market countries although it fell short of those recorded in 1959 (19 per cent) and in 1960 (25 per cent).[12] In June, 1962, Walter Hallstein stated that intra-Community trade had increased 73 per cent in four years.[13]

France is the Community's largest producer of grain, accounting for the production of about 45 per cent of the Community's wheat and 40 per cent of its coarse grains. Between "1951" and "1961" French grain production increased by 61 per cent. Germany, the largest wheat-deficit area within the Community, is also traditionally the largest importer of Syrian wheat. Generally speaking, the availability of cheaper French wheat is at the expense of Syrian wheat, which is subject to a larger levy. But this is true mainly of soft wheat whether one is speaking of French wheat in the German market or in the Italian market. The Common Market is generally a deficit area so far as durum or quality (hard) wheat is concerned. As the result of progress already made in the development of new varieties of durum wheat in Italy and southern France, these countries may step up their production of durum wheat.[14] The ever-in-

---

[11] *Bulletin from the European Community*, August, 1960, p. 4.

[12] EEC Commission, *Fifth General Report on the Activities of the Community* (1 May 1961—30 April 1962), (n.p., 1962), p. 95.

[13] *Bulletin of the European Economic Community*, August, 1962, p. 6.

[14] U.S. Department of Agriculture, *Impact of Common Market Proposals on Competitive Status of U.S. Bread and Feed Grains in the EEC Area* (Washington, October, 1961), p. 8.

creasing intra-Community trade coupled with the phenomenal expansion of production and the introduction and development of
new varieties could adversely affect the exports of Syrian wheat to
the Common Market countries during the transition period.

The same could be true of Iraqi barley exports. France, which
is already the biggest producer of food in Western Europe, has
recently embarked on a program to step up output even more. The
program which is now in operation calls for an over-all production
increase of 30 per cent by 1965 as compared with output in 1959.
The largest increases are sought for grain, especially for barley and
some other products. France is already the most important exporter of barley to the other Common Market countries. In 1961,
for example, it exported barley worth nearly $40,000,000 to the
EEC.[15] Should the new program of agricultural modernization be
implemented effectively, the rate of French barley exports to other
EEC countries may well increase far beyond the present level.

The effects of the Common Market on Syrian wheat and Iraqi
barley during the second period, namely, after 1970, are even
more difficult to assess. By 1970 the existing levy system will be
abolished. As a result, intra-Community trade will be unimpeded
by any levy. On the other hand, the Common Market will present the outside world, including the Middle East, with a uniform
levy system linked to prices which will have been leveled out by
1970. Whether this single system will be protectionist or not will
depend on the level of grain prices at the time.[16] However, the fact
remains that the Community's current agricultural policy may affect outside suppliers in two ways. First, the progressive increase in
grain prices will probably lead to higher levies on barley and wheat
by 1970. Second, the increasing prices during the transition period
will probably bring more land under grain cultivation and hence

[15] Statistical Office of the European Communities, *Foreign Trade Statistics:
Analytical Tables—Imports, January–December 1961* (Brussels, 1962).
[16] Official Spokesman of the Commission, EEC, *The Common Agricultural Policy
—Protectionist or Liberal?* (Brussels, 1962), p. 3.

augment the EEC's own production to such an extent that Middle East exports of barley may be partly or wholly shut off from the Common Market after 1970. So far as wheat is concerned, the Common Market may adversely affect the importation of soft wheat, which is already grown in near-sufficient amounts in the Market area. Hard wheat will probably continue to be needed even after the complete establishment of a common market in 1970.

RICE

Another major Middle East grain which has to be considered is rice. The only Middle East country that has fairly consistently exported rice to the Common Market countries in the past is Egypt. Of the six Common Market countries, West Germany, the Netherlands, Belgium, and Luxembourg have imported Egyptian rice, but Germany's share has been far the largest. In 1954, for example, Egypt exported 1,775 metric tons of rice to Germany for $260,000 and in 1956 the amount and value increased to 18,796 tons and $2,127,000. Egypt's total exports to EEC countries in 1956 amounted to $95,728,000, and the value of its total rice exports to the world reached $25,000,000.[17]

The Common Market has not yet officially approved regulations for the rice sector of its agricultural policy. But draft regulations have been drawn up, and the similarity between these and the regulations for wheat and barley can be discerned. On February 22, 1962, the European Parliament rendered its opinion, in the form of a resolution, on a common rice policy. Prior to this resolution the Commission had referred the matter to the Economic and Social Committee, which approved the Commission's proposal for a common policy for rice.[18] In February, 1962, however, the EEC Council withdrew its proposed rice regulations and instructed a group of experts to draw up a new draft.

[17] See Table 15.   [18] EEC, *Fifth General Report*, p. 164.

On May 7, 1962, the Commission proposed regulations to the Council for the progressive establishment of a common rice market. These regulations are largely based upon those for the cereals discussed previously. The rice market, however, presents certain special features, and therefore differences are needed between these regulations and those for other cereals. The fundamental differences are that there are only two rice-producing countries in the Community—France and Italy—and that there are no barriers to trade in rice in the other four member states except in Germany, where a customs duty is imposed on paddy rice and milled rice. For this reason it is provided that a single market in rice is to be established in the four countries. This will make it possible to provide for the fixing, in the four countries, of a common threshold price, a single c.i.f. price, and a uniform levy on imports from third countries.[19]

The common organization of the market in rice will apply to rice in husk or husked but still enclosed in the pericarp, to the whole grain ground to remove the pericarp, whether or not polished or glazed, to broken rice, and to rice starch. The threshold price will be set annually by the Council. The criterion applied when this is first fixed will be stabilization of the price of rice at a level equal to the average price of imports during the last twelve months for which statistics are available. The threshold price for broken rice is to be equal to that for rice, less an identical percentage for each member state. The levy for nonmember countries will be equal to the difference between the threshold price and the c.i.f. price.

No matter what shape the ultimate regulations may take, it is certain that the basic principles embodied in the twenty-seven-article proposal just mentioned will be applied to rice imports from countries outside the Common Market. The levy here, as in the case of other cereals, will be high, as it will be based on the difference between high threshold prices and the lowest c.i.f. price. At

[19] For the full text of the regulation on the progressive establishment of a common rice market, see Suppl. to *Bull. of EEC*, No. 7, 1962, pp. 25–36.

the same time the importation of rice (including broken rice) into a nonproducer member state from another member state will not be subject to any levy whatsoever.[20] Thus with rice as with other cereals, trade among member states as contrasted with trade with nonmember states must be preferentially treated in compliance with the general principles set forth in the Treaty of Rome and the proposed implementing regulations. One observer has stated that "in the transition period this levy would reduce rice imports since it would permit consumer prices to go up about 30 to 40 per cent." [21]

High levies during the transition period will not be the only factor discouraging the export of Egyptian rice to Common Market countries. Two other factors must be considered. One is the intra-Community trade in rice at the expense of outside suppliers. This question comes up because the draft proposals for a common agricultural policy for rice have indicated that the basic aim is to establish a common rice market having the characteristics of a domestic market. This objective is to be attained by guiding production to meet requirements, maintaining profitable levels of return for producers, and supporting the interests of processors, traders, and the buying public. These proposals were apparently based on the assumption that rice is rice no matter what its shape, size, or cooking behavior may be. This led to the conclusion that, inasmuch as the total over-all production of rice in Italy and France is roughly equal to present consumption, this production could be expected, or adjusted, to supply all the rice needed for food. Theoretically only broken rice for industrial use would be a consistent import.[22]

Should self-sufficiency in rice within the Common Market materialize to any significant degree, it may well be expected that outside suppliers, including the Egyptians, will suffer. But the in-

[20] *Ibid.*, Art. 2.

[21] U.S. Department of Agriculture, *Foreign Agriculture*, March 25, 1963, p. 8.

[22] *Ibid.*, March 11, 1963, p. 3.

dications are that this will hardly be the case because neither France nor Italy produces the long-grain varieties that many consumers in the Common Market prefer to buy. This is not unrelated to the fact that for the five-year period 1957–61 Italy's shipments to EEC countries averaged only about 25,000 tons a year. But as we have just seen, in 1956 Egypt's exports of rice to West Germany alone amounted to nearly 19,000 tons. This fact, however, does not necessarily mean that Egypt will continue to export more rice to the EEC countries than will Italy. In 1961, for example, Italy's exports of rice to the EEC amounted to $2,631,000 while Egypt's were $2,319,000.[23]

Furthermore, the development of trade between the Common Market and the associated states of Africa may adversely affect the exports of Egyptian rice to EEC countries. Article 132(1) of the Treaty of Rome provides that "Member States shall, in their commercial exchanges with the countries and territories [of Africa], apply the same rules which they apply among themselves pursuant to this Treaty." Article 133(1) of the Treaty provides that "imports originating in the countries or territories [of Africa] shall, on their entry into Member States, benefit by the total abolition of customs duties which shall take place progressively between Member States in conformity with the provisions of this Treaty." The Implementing Convention which has been in force for a period of five years and is soon to be replaced by a new convention embodies these general principles of the Treaty.[24]

This means that the associated African states are enjoying the same reduction of customs duties as the Common Market countries themselves, with the result that exports of African agricultural products including rice to the Common Market countries are growing. By January 1, 1962, the tariff on nonliberalized agricul-

---

[23] Statistical Office of the European Communities, *op. cit.*

[24] A typescript of the Implementation Convention was made available to me by the European Community Information Service, Washington, D.C.

tural products had been reduced 35 per cent and on liberalized agricultural products 30 per cent. As a result the value of the Community's imports from the associated countries rose 6 per cent over that for the first quarter of 1960, which was 3 per cent above that of 1959.

This upward trend in the exports of agricultural products is expected to gain momentum after the conclusion of the new convention between the Common Market and the associated countries of Africa.[25] To cite an example, in 1961 the value of Madagascar's exports of rice to the Common Market was greater than those of Egypt or even of Italy. Egypt's rice exports to EEC countries in that year were worth $2,319,000, Italy's $2,631,000, and Madagascar's $4,014,000.[26] If this trend continues—as is likely—it is bound to affect the Egyptian rice exports to the Common Market countries.

Thus exports of Egyptian rice to Common Market countries may be adversely affected in three different but related ways. The levy system envisaged in the draft proposals, if implemented, will increase the tariff on Egyptian rice. The intra-Community trade in rice may decrease the imports of Egyptian rice. And, finally, the favorable treatment accorded rice imports from the associated countries of Africa may also result in a progressive decrease in imports from Egypt and after 1970 may cut them off altogether.

[25] EEC, *Fifth General Report*, pp. 197–98.
[26] Statistical Office of the European Communities, *op. cit.*

III

The Vegetable and Fruit Sector

THE regulations of the Common Market have already made themselves felt on Middle East exports of vegetables and fruit, and they have been particularly serious for fruit exports. The principal exporters of fresh and dried fruits are the non-Arab countries of Iran, Israel, and Turkey. Their exports have not only been subjected to a progressively higher tariff but are threatened by a number of protective measures, by increasing trade within the Market countries, and by the association of Greece with the EEC. The future effects on Middle East fruits will probably be even more serious unless the current attempts of the non-Arab countries at reaching various forms of accommodation with EEC prove successful.

MIDDLE EAST EXPORTS TO
THE COMMON MARKET

The two major exporters of vegetables to Common Market countries are Egypt and Lebanon. Egypt's vegetable exports to Market countries amounted to $1,880,000 in 1952, to $2,958,000 in 1954, and to $6,724,000 in 1956. In 1956 Egypt's world vegetable exports were worth $18,000,000, over one-third of which went to Common Market countries. West Germany was Egypt's best customer. Lebanon's exports to the Market countries amounted, in the same years, to $146,000, $2,015,000, and $1,041,000. In 1956 Lebanon's world total of vegetable exports was valued at $6,500,000, and over $1,000,000 worth went to the Common Market countries. Lebanon's best customer was France.[1]

Fruit exports to Common Market countries have been far more important than vegetable or grain exports. To take fresh fruits first, five major exporters are involved. These are Iran, Israel, Lebanon, Iraq, and Turkey. Iran's exports to the Common Market countries amounted to $496,000 in 1952, $593,000 in 1954, and $10,534,000 in 1956. In the same years Israel's exports amounted to $1,845,000, $6,847,000, and $10,534,000; Lebanon's to $615,000, $159,000, and $542,000; and Iraq's to $274,000, $1,087,000, and $1,150,000. Turkey, however, exported the most fruit in those years. Its exports were valued at $10,457,000, $12,699,000, and $18,694,000. Germany was the most important customer for Iran, Lebanon, Iraq, Turkey, and Israel. Germany was closely followed by France as Israel's second most important customer. And France was Lebanon's most important customer for fresh fruits, as for vegetables.[2]

The two leading exporters of dried fruits to the Common Market countries are Iran and Turkey. Iran's dried fruit exports amounted to $4,491,000 in 1952, $5,377,000 in 1954, and $8,162,000 in 1956. In the same years Turkish exports amounted to $8,001,000, $6,459,000, and $7,295,000. Germany has been the most important Common Market customer for both Iran and Turkey, although Turkish exports of dried fruits are spread more evenly among Common Market countries than are those of Iran. Since the establishment of the Common Market, Iran's exports of dried fruits

---

[1] See Tables 15 and 19.   [2] See Tables 16–19, 21.

have decreased but Turkey's exports have increased phenomenally. Iran's exports amounted to over $8,000,000 in 1956 but decreased to less than $6,000,000 in 1961. During the same period Turkish exports practically doubled, going from about $7,000,000 to nearly $14,000,000.[3]

Establishment of the Common Market in the vegetable and fruit sector, as in other sectors, envisages a transition period which will expire on December 31, 1969. From 1970 onward the Common Market in vegetables and fruit, as in other commodities, will presumably be in full effect. Analysis of the implications of the common market in vegetables and fruit for Middle Eastern products will therefore require examination of transitional as well as final measures. For analytical purposes these measures may be conveniently examined under four major categories, hence the four subheadings that follow.

"QUALITY STANDARDS"

"Quality standards" is one of the major devices used in the regulation of the common market in vegetables and fruit. These standards are to be applied progressively in the intra-Community trade and in the trade of Common Market countries with the rest of the world. Products from third countries may be acceptable for import into the Common Market only if the Common Market's standards of quality or "standards that are at least equivalent" [4] have been applied to them. These standards have been applied to vegetables and fruit since July 1, 1962. However, the Commission was given the responsibility of setting forth by the end of 1962 the

[3] Statistical Office of the European Communities, *Foreign Trade Statistics: Analytical Tables—Imports, January–December 1961* (Brussels, 1962).
[4] See Art. 2 of Regulation No. 23 in EEC Commission, *Regulations and Decisions in the Field of Agriculture Adopted by the Council on 14 January 1962* (n.p., n.d.).

conditions, methods, and timetable for applying the standards. The quality standards must be fully applied not later than January 1, 1968.[5]

The Council of the EEC has decided upon two categories of products to which the standards of quality should be applied. The first category includes cauliflower, lettuce, onions, tomatoes, apples other than cider apples, pears, apricots, peaches, and plums. The second category includes spinach, chicory (white), peas, beans, carrots, artichokes, sweet oranges, tangerines, clementines, lemons, dessert grapes, cherries, and strawberries. At the time that the Council specified these products, it also laid down the standards of quality for the first category, each product of this category being subject to a set of requirements separately drawn up. The common standards of quality for onions, for example, should apply to all onions of the species *Allium cepa* L. except "silver skin" onions and green onions with all their leaves. Minimum requirements for onions are that the bulbs must be (a) whole, (b) sound, (c) clean and, in particular, free from all residue of fertilizer or other treatment, (d) free from frost damage, (e) dry enough for the use intended, (f) free from abnormal external moisture, and (g) free from any extraneous smell or taste; (h) the stalk must be twisted or cut off clean and must be not more than 4 centimeters long (except for onions in strings).[6]

The quality standards for the first category (Annex 1A of Regulation No. 23) must be fully applied not later than January 1, 1965. This includes onions whether traded within the Community or imported from outside. On this basis, beginning January 1, 1965, Egyptian onions entering their long-established German markets will be subject to these new quality standards. Once the quality standards for other vegetables and fruits are determined by the Council, they will also apply to Middle East vegetables and fresh fruits. There is no sure way of predicting exactly how the applica-

[5] *Ibid.*, Art. 3.   [6] *Ibid.*

tion of Common Market quality standards will affect Middle Eastern exporters of vegetables and fruits. These standards together with the sizing, marking, and packing requirements of the Market might well have salutary effects upon the lax packing practices of some Middle Eastern countries.

"ELIMINATION OF QUANTITATIVE RESTRICTIONS"

Progressive elimination of quantitative restrictions during the transition period is one of the measures specified by the Treaty of Rome for the gradual establishment of the Common Market.[7] EEC countries have prohibited quantitative restrictions in their trade relations in general. Restrictions on industrial products have already been abolished, but agricultural products have been subject to special arrangements. One of these special arrangements governs the vegetable and fruit sector as specified in Article 9 of the pertinent regulations of the Community.[8]

The specific vegetables and fruits for which quantitative restrictions are abolished were mentioned in the previous section of this chapter. However, the regulations provide for a timetable for this abolition of restrictions. The timetable is based upon the classification of products, which are listed as "Extra," "Class 1," and "Class 2." Quantitative restrictions on the products falling within the "Extra" class were to be abolished not later than June 30, 1962; those falling under Class 1 not later than December 31, 1963, and those under Class 2 must be abolished not later than December 31, 1965.[9]

Under the Treaty of Rome, if the progressive abolition of quantitative restrictions proved harmful, the member state affected could resort to a system of minimum prices below which imports could be temporarily suspended, reduced, or made conditional on

[7] See Arts. 30–37 of the Treaty of Rome.   [8] See EEC, *Regulations.*
[9] *Ibid.*, No. 23, Art. 9(2).

their price being above the minimum price fixed for the product concerned.[10] Under the regulations on vegetables and fruits the EEC countries undertook to cease to claim the benefit of the minimum price device. Instead, if liberalization of imports should prove harmful, the member state affected may resort to certain "safeguard measures," including the closing of its borders to importation. But "all safeguard measures affecting trade between Member States must first have been applied to relations with third countries, the principle of Community preference being respected." [11]

Thus the abolition of quantitative restrictions, which may seem on the surface to be concerned only with the intra-Community trade, is not without significant implications for third countries. Should the abolition of such measures, for example, appear to jeopardize the interests of the producers or consumers of vegetables and fruits in a given Common Market country, before any safeguard measure is taken by that country vis-à-vis the imports from the other Common Market countries it must take such measures, including the closing of its borders, with regard to imports from third countries, including those of the Middle East. Furthermore, the exporters of Middle East vegetables and fruits, like the exporters of any other outsider, may suddenly find their exports suspended or subjected to a "countervailing charge" if their prices fall below "a reference price" within the Community.[12] The reference price is calculated on the average quotations recorded over a certain period on the producer markets in the Community where price levels are the lowest for products of Community origin and for a specified standard of quality. The countervailing charge that a third country may have to pay is based upon the difference between the reference price and the price of the imported product at entry, excluding customs duties.[13]

---

[10] See Art. 44 of the Treaty of Rome.

[11] EEC, *Regulations*, No. 23, Art. 10(5).

[12] *Ibid.*, Art. 11(2).　　　　　　　　[13] *Ibid.*, Art. 11.

REDUCTION OF CUSTOMS DUTIES

A far more significant way in which Middle East exporters of vegetables and fruit to the Common Market are affected is the progressive abolition of customs duties among the EEC countries. Under the Treaty of Rome the Common Market countries have generally undertaken (*a*) to abolish progressively in their trade relations customs duties in force and (*b*) to refrain from introducing any new customs duties.[14] In respect of each product, the basic duty which shall be subject to the successive reductions is the duty applied on January 1, 1957.[15] The Treaty also provides for a timetable for the reduction of customs duties. Three reductions are envisaged by the Treaty during the first stage of the transition period, three more in the course of the second stage, and the remaining during the third or the last stage of the transition period. The first stage began on January 1, 1958, and ended on December 31, 1961. The third reduction stipulated by the Treaty for the end of the first stage of the transition period was made on the latter date. The Treaty requires that the reduction applied to the duties on each product should amount to at least 25 per cent of the basic duty at the end of the first stage.[16] But acceleration of the implementation of the Treaty as a result of the decisions of the Council brought about far greater tariff reductions in the first stage of the transition period than were foreseen by the Treaty. By the end of the first stage the Common Market countries had brought the level of duties down to 60 per cent of the basic duty for industrial products, 65 per cent for nonliberalized agricultural products, and 70 per cent for liberalized agricultural products.[17]

The effect of the progressive reduction of customs duties on the

[14] *Ibid.*, Arts. 12 and 13.   [15] *Ibid.*, Art. 14.   [16] *Ibid.*, Art. 14(6).
[17] EEC Commission, *Fifth General Report on the Activities of the Community* (1 May 1961—30 April 1962), (n.p., 1962), p. 30.

imports of Middle East vegetables and fruits may be viewed from two different angles. One involves the reduction of customs duties among the Common Market countries themselves, and the other the association of Greece with the Common Market. To take the intra-Community reductions first, it must be realized that the magnitude of the impact will depend upon the Community's own capacity to produce such products, upon its consumption, and, in the last analysis, upon the degree of its self-sufficiency. Germany in 1958–59 was 85.4 per cent self-sufficient in fresh fruit. France was 81 per cent; Italy, 128.3 per cent; the Netherlands, 116.8 per cent; and Belgium and Luxembourg, 102.6 per cent. The percentages of self-sufficiency in vegetables for the same countries in the same period and in that same order were 77.2, 99.7, 99.1, 119.2, 156.5, and 104.9. For vegetables the Netherlands and Italy rank high in self-sufficiency; for fruits major increases have occurred in France, Italy, and Germany, but the greatest percentage increases have been in Belgium and the Netherlands.[18]

The significant degree of self-sufficiency in vegetables and fruits achieved in the Common Market countries, plus the ever-increasing reduction of customs duties among them, is bound to affect the exports of the Middle East countries. For example, Israeli citrus fruit exports have already been harmed, and there is every reason to believe that as the internal trade in fruits gains momentum the injury will be aggravated. According to Levi Eshkol, Israel's Finance Minister, "Until January 1, 1962, Germany had levied a 20% tariff on Israel's citrus products, and a tariff of only 16% on the same products imported from Italy; but on January 1, when the EEC entered the second stage of its transition period, the tariff for Israel was raised to 21% and that for Italy was reduced to 14%. In January 1961, the differential is liable to be in-

---

[18] EEC Commission, *Proposals for the Working Out and Putting into Effect of the Common Agricultural Policy in Application of Article 43 of the Treaty Establishing the European Economic Community* (Brussels, 1960), Part III, pp. 1–6.

creased to 12%."[19] This is bound to increase Italy's already enormous exports of fresh fruits to other Common Market countries at the expense of outside exporters of such products, including Israel. In 1961 alone Italy's exports of fresh fruits to EEC amounted to over $200,000,000; Israel's was over $13,000,000.[20]

The effects of lowered tariffs in intra-Community trade are not, of course, confined to Israel or to exports of fresh fruits. All of the Middle Eastern countries that export fruit or vegetables to the EEC feel them, although they have not as yet been publicly assessed.

To aid future assessment of these effects it may be well to indicate the value of Middle East exports of these commodities in 1961, the final year of the first stage of the transition period and the year just preceding the establishment of the common policy in vegetables and fruits. In 1961 Egypt exported vegetables worth $7,013,000 and Lebanon $14,000 to the Common Market countries. In the same year exports of fresh fruits from Iran, Lebanon, Iraq, and Turkey amounted to $742,000, $61,000, $273,000, and $18,694,000, respectively.[21] It must be noted that these figures represent the value of the exports of these countries in these commodities after several internal tariff cuts had already taken place.

The other way by which Middle East exports of vegetables and fruits to the EEC may be affected is through the association of Greece with the Market. The Greek economy is mainly agricultural, and in the vegetable and particularly in the fruit sector it is significantly competitive with the Middle East. For this reason Israel, Turkey, and Iran have cause for concern. The association of Greece with the Common Market places its exports in a decidedly favorable position.

[19] "Israel's Economic Situation," *International Financial News Survey,* November 7, 1962, pp. 376–77.
[20] Statistical Office of the European Communities, *op. cit.* [21] *Ibid.*

On June 8, 1959, the Greek government requested that Greece be associated with the EEC. Apparently, Greece chose association rather than membership because it "deemed it advisable to advance [toward final integration] at a somewhat more deliberate pace than that adopted among the Six." The reason for the choice of a more deliberate pace was "precisely the difference in level of development between Greece and the Six." [22] After exploratory talks with the EEC Commission in September, 1959, formal negotiations began in March, 1960, and the definitive Agreement of Association was concluded in Athens on July 9, 1961. The instruments of ratification were exchanged on August 24, 1962, and the Agreement came into force on November 1, 1962.[23]

Although the Athens Agreement reflects this "deliberate pace," it should not be assumed that the pace of the Greek association is so deliberate that its effects are to be felt only in the future. The customs duties between Greece and the EEC are to be abolished gradually over a twelve-year period beginning with the entry into force of the Agreement on November 1, 1962. But the EEC made an exception to this basic timetable which is of particular significance to our discussion here. The exception is that the Common Market countries cut their tariffs on imports from Greece as soon as the Agreement went into force. The level of the cut was the same as had been reached through successive reductions within the Community. Furthermore, future internal tariff reductions were made applicable to Greek goods.

The application of these tariff reductions to fruit and vegetable imports from Greece will place the Middle East exports of these commodities at a progressive disadvantage. It is true that the Community has reserved the right to resort to safeguard measures restricting imports of Greek citrus fruits, dessert grapes, peaches,

---

[22] For details see *Bulletin of the European Economic Community*, September, 1962, pp. 7–14.

[23] See EEC Commission, *Accord créant une association entre la Communauté économique européenne et la Grèce et documents annexes* (n.p., February, 1962).

and so forth should they rise beyond an agreed level. But the fact still remains that Greek exports of these commodities are subject to an ever-decreasing level of customs duties as contrasted with Middle East fruit exports. Furthermore, it should be noted that with respect to certain products the Community has lowered its duties on Greek imports ahead of the normal timetable. For example, lower duties are at present applied to Greek raisins, which are one of the most important items in the traditional exports of Iran to the Common Market countries.

The Greek association will probably prove increasingly disadvantageous to the Middle East's two leading exporters of dried fruits, namely, Iran and Turkey. The value of the dried fruit exports by these countries to the six European countries before the establishment of the Common Market has already been given (see pp. 36–37). It is too early at the moment to determine the impact of the Greek association with the Common Market countries on the exports of Iran and Turkey. But for future assessment it may be useful to indicate the value of their exports in the year just preceding the Greek Agreement. Iran's exports of dried fruits to the EEC in 1961 were worth nearly $6,000,000, and Turkey's exports nearly $14,000,000. In the same year Greek exports were nearly $10,000,-000.[24] But as was mentioned earlier, the challenge of the Greek association is not confined to dried fruits. In 1961 Greek exports of fresh fruits to the EEC countries amounted to more than $9,000,000. The Agreement of Association may well result in a progressive increase in this amount in spite of the existence of an agreed level of imports in respect to certain products.

ESTABLISHMENT OF A COMMON EXTERNAL TARIFF

A fourth measure by which the Middle East exports of vegetables and fruits will be affected by the Common Market is the

[24] Statistical Office of the European Communities, *op. cit.*

establishment of a common customs tariff. This measure is closely related to the one just discussed. As internal customs duties are progressively reduced, the six member countries work toward the attainment of a common external tariff system. Generally speaking, the six countries have already taken steps toward that end. On January 1, 1961, they moved their national tariffs 30 per cent closer to the common external tariff. Another adjustment of 30 per cent will take place on December 31, 1965. Thus the gap between the national tariffs and the common external tariff will then be reduced by 60 per cent, and, of course, there is a possibility that the Council may decide to speed matters.[25]

Article 8(2) of Regulation No. 23 makes the progressive alignment of the national tariffs applicable to the vegetable and fruit sector. Although by 1970 the customs duties among the member states will have been abolished, the member states will then present third countries with a uniform tariff system in respect to fruit and vegetables. The tariff on each product has been agreed upon by the EEC countries in List F attached to the Treaty of Rome. To cite a few examples, vegetables, fresh or chilled, will have 12 percent ad valorem duties. The duties on dried, dehydrated, or evaporated vegetables, whole, cut, sliced, broken, or in powder, but not further prepared, will be 20 per cent on onions and 16 per cent on others. For citrus fruits the rate ranges from 8 per cent on lemons to 15 or 20 per cent on oranges (depending on the season).

What this will do to Israeli exports, for example, is not hard to see. By 1970 its major export item, citrus fruit, will face a 20 per cent duty as compared with a current German tariff of 10 per cent and a Benelux tariff of 13 per cent.[26] And at the same time Italian citrus fruits will be made available to the entire Community without any duties.

[25] EEC Commission, *Fifth General Report*, pp. 24, 36–37.
[26] *Near East Report*, March 13, 1962, p. 23.

Whether it is Egyptian onions, Israeli citrus, Iranian raisins, Turkish figs, or Iraqi dates, the full impact of the Common Market on the exports of the Middle East will not be felt until 1970. But in the meantime as quality standards are gradually applied, as intra-Community trade is accelerated through the abolition of quantitative restrictions and the reduction of customs duties, and as the common external tariff is gradually approximated, Middle East exporters of vegetables and fruits will find themselves confronted with an emerging economic union which is guided in part by the "principle of Community preference" in its dealings with the rest of the world.

IV

Other Major Exports of the Middle East

OTHER major exports of the Middle East to the EEC countries are cotton, tobacco, and carpets. No challenge to the cotton exports of Egypt or of other Middle East countries is posed by the quota or tariff policy of the Common Market, although the association of Greece and the African states with the EEC may create competition for Middle East exporters. So far as tobacco and rugs are concerned, the non-Arab countries have again borne the brunt of the EEC changes. Turkey is the Middle East's principal exporter of tobacco to the Common Market, and Iran is the main exporter of rugs. Unless the efforts of these countries to reach agreement with EEC prove successful, the impact of the Common Market on the export of these commodities will probably be even more serious in future than it is now.

This chapter will confine itself to cotton, tobacco, and rugs because these items, with oil, fruits, and vegetables, already discussed, constitute the major exports of the Middle East to the EEC. In 1961, for example, most of the Middle East countries included in this study exported many groups of products totaling over 120 in number but having very little value in comparison with the few major items.[1] Egypt exported fifty-six groups of products, ranging from furniture and fixtures to aluminum, but they were negligible in value as compared with cotton, rice, and vegetables. Iran, to cite another example, exported a total of thirty-two groups of products, ranging from hay and fodder to oil seeds, but they were insignificant as compared with dried fruits and rugs, not to mention crude oil and petroleum products. Examples could easily be multiplied, but these should suffice.

COTTON

Of the three products just mentioned cotton is most important in the sense that a number of Middle East countries have traditionally been exporters of cotton to the Common Market countries. The major exporters are Egypt, Turkey, Iran, and Syria. Egypt's exports of cotton to Market countries in 1952 amounted to over $126,000,000, to over $109,000,000 in 1954, and to over $77,000,000 in 1956. This significant drop can be attributed in part to the unprecedentedly large exports of Egyptian cotton to Soviet bloc countries after the arms deal with Czechoslovakia in 1955. A general shift in Egypt's trade pattern occurred in the 1955–58 period, when its exports to the Soviet Union and other Eastern European countries rose from 19.4 per cent of the value of total exports in 1955 to 40 per cent in 1958.[2] In spite of the fact that the total value of its exports to the Soviet bloc was decreasing in 1960, exports of Egyptian cotton to the Common Market continued to decline, amounting to slightly over $41,000,000 in 1961.[3] Cotton is still, however, the single most important export of Egypt to the

---

[1] See, for example, the exports of these countries in 1961 in Statistical Office of the European Communities, *Foreign Trade Statistics: Analytical Tables—Imports, January–December 1961* (Brussels, 1962).

[2] UN, *Economic Developments of the Middle East, 1959–1961* (New York, 1962), p. 71.

[3] See Statistical Office of the European Communities, *op. cit.*

Common Market. In 1961 it constituted about half of the total value of Egypt's exports to the EEC.

A second important exporter of cotton to the Common Market is Turkey. In 1952 Turkey exported over $54,000,000, in 1954 over $26,000,000, and in 1956 over $22,000,000. In the last year Turkey's total cotton exports amounted to $27,000,000. The export of Turkish cotton to the Common Market reached a new high in 1961 when it rose to over $44,000,000.[4]

A third important cotton-exporting country of the Middle East is Syria. Syrian exports to the Common Market in 1952 amounted to more than $21,000,000, in 1954 to more than $26,000,000, and in 1956 to more than $30,000,000. In the last year all exports of Syrian cotton were $42,000,000.[5] In 1961, however, Syrian exports dropped to about $19,500,000.[6] Nevertheless, cotton was the single most important export of Syria to the Common Market countries.

Iran's cotton exports to the Market countries have been much smaller than those of the countries just discussed. In 1952 they were worth about $4,000,000, in 1954 they were worth more than twice as much, and in 1956 more than three times as much. In the last year the cotton exports constituted about a third of the value of the total exports of Iran to the Common Market countries (excluding petroleum). In 1961 they were about an eighth of the total (also excluding petroleum).

For the cotton of Egypt, Iran, and Syria, France has fairly consistently been the most important Common Market customer. Germany has been the second most important customer. In the case of Turkey, however, Germany rather than France has generally been the leading importer.

The implications of the Common Market for Middle East cotton exports may be viewed from two different angles. One is from the standpoint of the EEC's customs duties on imports of cotton.

---

[4] See Table 21.   [5] See Table 20.
[6] See Statistical Office of the European Communities, *op. cit.*

The EEC is the world's greatest market for cotton, importing seven-eighths of its needs. Obviously it has not achieved any significant degree of self-sufficiency. As might be expected, therefore, practically all cotton imports to Common Market countries are duty-free.[7] Only Italy charges a small duty of 4.2 per cent.[8] Nevertheless, Middle East exports of cotton to Italy were substantial before and have been since the establishment of the Common Market. The only significant exception to this has been Turkey, whose exports of cotton to Italy have generally been smaller than those of the other major cotton-exporting countries of the Middle East.[9] Thus to date the over-all situation has encouraged Middle East cotton exports to the six Common Market countries.

But is there any reason to believe that this will continue? From available evidence it would seem that the favorable conditions for Middle East cotton exports will not only continue during the transition period (before 1970) but will also gradually improve. In part this is because the Common Market has no plans for quota restrictions.[10] More important, however, is the fact that under the Treaty of Rome the common external tariff for cotton (cotton not carded or combed, cotton linters, raw cotton, and cotton waste) is nil.[11] This means that Middle East exports of these products will be duty-free after 1970. Furthermore, in the course of the transition period the Italian duty will be gradually reduced to zero. Thus, so far as quota restrictions and customs duties are concerned, the prospects for Middle East cotton exports to the Common Market are promising in the foreseeable future.

But a challenge to Middle East exports of cotton to the Common Market may emanate from factors other than quota restrictions or customs duties. This brings us to the second stand-

[7] See List F attached to the Treaty of Rome, Nos. 55.01 and ex 55.02 in the Brussels Nomenclature.

[8] U.S. Department of Agriculture, *Foreign Agriculture*, West European Issue, November, 1962, p. 15.

[9] See Table 21.

[10] *Bulletin from the European Community*, May, 1961, p. 7.

[11] See the Treaty of Rome, List F, Nos. 55.01 and ex 55.02.

point of consideration of the implications of the EEC for Middle East cotton exports—consideration of the competition from cotton-producing countries associated with the Common Market. These countries are Greece and some African states.

As an associate member Greece may one day become an important supplier of cotton to the Common Market. Cotton is by no means a new commodity in Greece, where cotton production flourished as early as the second century B.C. Yet for many centuries Greece's cotton output remained insignificant as compared with that of the Egyptians, who in the late 1800's borrowed many ideas for cotton from the Greeks. Since 1931, when the Greeks formulated a national policy for cotton, the output has increased phenomenally, changing Greece from a net importer of cotton to a net exporter. The gains in output began long before the association with the Common Market and were stimulated by such incentives as the provision of credit and seed and through acreage subsidies.[12] But with the association may come "preferential" treatment for Greece's cotton exports to the Common Market. Furthermore, Greece's own efforts at increasing cotton output may well be furthered by the financial aid that it is to receive from the Common Market for the protection and development of its economy in general. During the first five years under the Athens Agreement, Greece may obtain loans from the Community up to a total of $125,000,000, in accordance with the rules of the European Investment Bank.[13] In 1961 Greece's cotton exports to the Common Market amounted to slightly over $5,000,000, but in 1962, when the Athens Agreement went into effect, the exports increased to over $11,000,000.[14]

It is possible that Middle East cotton exports to the Common

[12] U.S. Department of Agriculture, *op. cit.*, p. 22.
[13] EEC, *Information Memo, Association with Greece* (Brussels, March, 1963), p. 4.
[14] Cf. *ibid.* and EEC, *Information Memo, Association with Greece* (Brussels, August, 1962), pp. 5–6.

Market may also be challenged by imports from the African associates, to which may be extended preferential treatment by the Market. Furthermore, the cotton output and hence exports of these countries may increase under the general impetus of Common Market financial aid to their agriculture. In the first five years of association, which expired in 1962, the African associates received a total of about $780,000,000 in aid; 18 per cent of this aid went into improvement of agriculture.[15] The new convention, which is soon to be signed, envisages an enlarged Development Fund, which will, among other things, provide aid for the continuing improvement of these countries' agriculture. Furthermore, the EEC will finance schemes that will allow the products of the associates to be marketed throughout the Community at competitive prices by encouraging the rational selection of crops and modification of sales methods and helping producers to make any changes necessary.[16] In 1961 together the Central African Republic and the Federal Republic of Cameroon exported over $9,000,000 worth of cotton to the Common Market countries.[17] These exports may well increase in the near future since the mutually beneficial ties between these countries and the Common Market will probably be further extended to their trade relations.

TOBACCO

The relationship between the Common Market and Turkish tobacco exports will be discussed from two standpoints. One is

[15] EEC Commission, *EEC Action in the Associated Countries,* address delivered to the African and Malagasy Economic Conference (Marseilles 18, 19 and 20 October 1962) by M. Jacques Ferrandi, Director of Research and Development Programmes in the Directorate General for Overseas Development (1243/pp/63-E), p. 22. See also EEC, *European Development Fund: Balance-Sheet 1958–1962* (Brussels, January, 1963; P-3/63-E).

[16] EEC, *Information Memo, Convention Associating the African States and Madagascar with the European Economic Community* (Brussels, December 21, 1962; PP 500/62-E), p. 3.

[17] See Statistical Office of the European Communities, *op. cit.*

the Community's degree of self-sufficiency and trade in tobacco. Germany, which is Turkey's largest market,[18] produces some 20,000 tons of tobacco and imports over 90,000 tons. Belgian production of leaf tobacco is some 10 per cent of the country's total consumption, which is particularly high (roughly 90 ounces per capita each year). Tobacco production in the Netherlands is negligible, while consumption is over 29,000 tons a year, practically all of it imported. The French tobacco output is 55,000 tons a year, supplemented by imports of 29,000 tons. Italy is the Common Market's largest tobacco producer. Its 60,000 tons are supplemented by 11,000 tons of imported tobacco.[19]

The Community's over-all deficiency in unmanufactured tobacco does not necessarily mean that intra-Community trade in tobacco will not increase. Such an increase will probably be made possible by Italy and the newly associated member, Greece. Italy's determination to maintain a strong trade relationship with other members of the EEC was exemplified in the first six months of 1962. During that period Italy itself imported 35,900,000 pounds of tobacco, reflecting the shortfall in the Italian crop in 1961. Nevertheless, it managed to export over 18,000,000 pounds to Germany and more than 2,000,000 pounds to the Netherlands.[20] A far more important challenge to Turkish tobacco exports to Common Market countries could come from the Community's imports from Greece. In 1961 Greece's tobacco exports to the Community amounted to more than $26,000,000. In 1962, when Greece became an associate member of the Community, its tobacco exports mounted to nearly $34,000,000.[21]

The other way in which Turkish tobacco exports could suffer is through the Community's high duty. The common external duty on unmanufactured tobacco was originally set at 30 per cent ad

---

[18] See Table 21.   [19] Bull. from Eur. Com., December, 1960, p. 15.

[20] U.S. Department of Agriculture, op. cit., January 21, 1963, pp. 11–12.

[21] Cf. EEC, Information Memo, Association with Greece (Brussels, March and August, 1963).

valorem. Later the Council decided to mitigate to some extent the effects of this duty by instituting a maximum and a minimum levy.[22] At the present time the common external tariff which will be fully effective by 1970 is set at 28 per cent ad valorem, with a maximum duty of 17.2 cents per pound and a minimum of 13.2 cents.[23]

The high duty on tobacco will have crucial effects because of Turkey's first Five-Year Plan (1963–67). This plan calls for a substantial increase in tobacco production. During the first year of the plan, tobacco production is set at almost 300,000,000 pounds, of which about 170,000,000 is expected to be exported during 1964. The plan further calls for production to approach 331,000,-000 pounds in 1967, of which about 183,000,000 pounds would be exported.[24] Fortunately Turkey's relentless efforts to join the EEC as an associate member will probably bear fruit in the near future. As a result of these efforts Turkey has apparently already reached a satisfactory agreement on its tobacco exports. It was reported in May, 1963, that the Common Market has agreed to open a duty-free quota for Turkish tobacco.[25]

RUGS

Iran is the leading Middle East exporter of rugs to the Common Market. In 1952 these exports amounted to nearly $3,000,000, in 1954 to nearly $7,000,000, and in 1956 to over $9,000,000. This consistent rise reached a new high in 1961, when Iran's rug exports to the Market countries rose to over $24,000,000. In that year Iran's total exports (excluding petroleum) to the EEC amounted to about $60,000,000.[26] The importance of rug exports for Iran is

[22] EEC Commission, *Fifth General Report on the Activities of the Community* (1 May 1961—30 April 1962), (n.p., 1962), p. 35.
[23] U.S. Department of Agriculture, *op. cit.*, November, 1962, p. 15.
[24] *Ibid.*, January 21, 1963, p. 11.
[25] *Bull. from Eur. Com.*, April–May, 1963, p. 17.   [26] Cf. Tables 9 and 16.

obvious, and the impact of the Common Market should not be difficult to assess.

Undoubtedly no increase in intra-Community trade could prove disadvantageous to Iran inasmuch as the six countries are not manufacturers of carpets that directly compete with Iran's exports. Some Iranian circles, however, have expressed concern over the possibility of competition from Turkish rugs if Turkey succeeds in becoming an associate member.[27] No attempt will be made to minimize the possible impact of such an eventuality, but Iran's fear of Turkish associate membership will probably be more justified in respect to Turkish exports other than rugs. Turkish exports of rugs to the Common Market countries have consistently been insignificant, to no small extent because Persian rugs are in far greater demand. Turkish rug exports to the EEC amounted to $310,000 in 1952, $119,000 in 1954, and $125,000 in 1956. In 1956 Turkey's total exports to the Common Market were worth more than $300,000,000.

The Common Market will affect Iran's rug exports chiefly through the common external tariff. At present this tariff is high if calculated rigidly on the basis of the terms of the Treaty of Rome.[28] If the final tariff should prove exorbitant, it might shut off Persian rugs partly or wholly from the Common Market by 1970. It will also progressively increase the duties on Persian rugs during the transition period, while the member countries step by step approximate the common external tariff.[29]

[27] *Ettela't Havai*, August 2, 1962, p. 3.

[28] See Articles 19 and 20 of the Treaty of Rome and List A attached to the Treaty.

[29] However, it appears that as a result of negotiations between the government of Iran and the EEC an understanding between the two parties has been reached and an agreement has been initialed. For detailed information see the section on Iran's reaction to the EEC in Chapter VI.

V

Consequences of Possible British Entry
into the Common Market

S HOULD Great Britain enter the Common Market, the exports of the Middle East countries would suffer even more
seriously because of the importance of British markets for Middle
East exporters. Britain's entry into the Common Market would
most seriously affect the same non-Arab countries of the Middle
East which are now chiefly bearing the brunt of the EEC impact.
In the absence of any agreement between Israel and the Common
Market before the entry of Britain, the exports of Israeli citrus
fruits could suffer seriously if Britain joined the EEC. The exports
of Turkish tobacco would suffer similarly if Turkey should fail to
become an associate member of the EEC.

In spite of the fact that since 1961 the European Parliament has
adopted six resolutions urging the accession of Great Britain to the
Common Market, the unilateral action of France in January, 1963,
resulted in the suspension of negotiations between the Common
Market and Britain. In deploring the action of France, Sicco
Mansholt, the Vice President of the European Economic Community, stated that in breaking off the EEC-British negotiations

President de Gaulle had set his own concept of a "continental Europe" against the concept of the New Europe cast within a framework of European institutions with a federal character.[1]

The interruption of the negotiations was not criticized by Mansholt alone. The European Parliament devoted two days of its plenary session held on February 4–8, 1963, to a political debate on the accession of the United Kingdom to the Community and the causes of the breakoff. In the course of these debates grave concern over the French action was expressed not only by some of the Ministers of Foreign Affairs of the Common Market countries but also by the representatives of the High Authority of the European Coal and Steel Community and the Euratom Commission.

In a dispassionate yet strong statement J. M. A. H. Luns, the Foreign Minister of the Netherlands, deplored the abrupt and surprising manner in which the French government had acted unilaterally in complete disregard of the wishes of all its partners. He stated in unequivocal terms: "For the Netherlands, Europe is not a continental Europe from which Britain is to be excluded. Britain has been, is, and always will be an integral part of Europe." [2]

Piero Malvestiti, President of the High Authority of the ECSC, stated that the High Authority had always considered that the presence of Great Britain in the ECSC would mean a strengthening of Europe. The Association Agreement of 1954, he stated, was a demonstration; it had helped to maintain cordial relations with Great Britain pending the latter's application for membership. A representative of the Euratom Commission also regretted the suspension of negotiations since it prevented further talks in the atomic energy field. He hoped that closer and more comprehensive

---

[1] This statement was made during Mansholt's visit to the United States (see *Bulletin from the European Community*, April–May, 1963, p. 4). For a devastating criticism of General de Gaulle's attitude, see the excellent article of Paul-Henri Spaak, "Hold Fast," *Foreign Affairs*, July, 1963, pp. 611–20.

[2] For details see *Bulletin of the European Economic Community*, March, 1963, pp. 9–10.

cooperation would ensue from the fruitful relations which had developed between the Community and the United Kingdom since the beginning of 1959.[3]

The "crisis of confidence" that French obstructionism had created within the European Economic Community also perturbed various political groups. The representative of the Christian-Democrat group of the Netherlands favored a United States of Europe which would be an open community closely linked with the free Atlantic world. His group had no desire to see any independent and neutral third force growing up and was against any kind of hegemony. The Socialist group of Germany stated that the Community must be sovereign and must prevent one or more of its members from gaining preponderance. Maurice Faure, speaking for the Liberal group, found the action of the French government to be contrary to the European spirit and believed it to be wrong to cut off Britain by a kind of outright veto for political reasons. He hoped for a Europe with the highest possible degree of autonomy, but he also believed that if international tensions were to be reduced and discussions with Moscow rendered possible the free world needed to show a united attitude and solidarity in its relations with the rest of the world.[4]

In spite of the intransigent French position one cannot escape the impression that support for the eventual membership of Great Britain is strong indeed, both within and outside the Community.[5] It would be sheer pessimism to conclude from the current position of France that the British are barred from entry into the Community forever. The experience of the European Defense Community should temper one's discouragement: the failure to establish it as the result of French action gave rise to a momentous series of events furthering the cause of European integration. Further-

[3] *Ibid.*   [4] *Ibid.*, pp. 11–12.
[5] See *Bull. from Eur. Com.*, April–May, 1963, p. 4, and Spaak in *Foreign Affairs*, July, 1963, pp. 611–20.

more, as Mansholt put it, "Whatever the policy of the French Government today, it was France that provided the initial inspiration toward a unified Europe." [6]

Trade between Britain and the Middle East is centuries old, but it decreased in recent decades. The Second World War in particular reduced British trade with the Middle East. By 1950–51, however, the prewar pattern of Middle East trade had been restored, and Britain as well as Western Europe had once again become one of the area's major trade partners. The only significant change in the old pattern was the relatively high level of imports from the United States.

Obviously the percentage of trade with Britain differs from country to country, but the over-all picture has been one of substantial commerce. In 1950, for example, Egyptian imports from the United Kingdom amounted to more than $100,000,000, while its total imports were slightly over $600,000,000. In the same year Egyptian exports to the United Kingdom amounted to more than $100,000,000, while its total exports were slightly over $500,000,-000. To cite another example, Iran's imports from Britain in the same year amounted to over $54,000,000 out of a total of about $190,000,000. Iranian exports to Britain in 1950 were worth more than $20,000,000 out of a total of about $100,000,000. Other Middle East countries such as Iraq, Israel, Syria, and Turkey have also traded substantially with the United Kingdom.[7]

In the period after 1950 British–Middle East trade suffered significantly, in part as a result of a number of political difficulties. The Anglo-Egyptian differences over evacuation of the Suez Canal and the Anglo-Iranian dispute over the nationalization of the Anglo-Iranian Oil Company were not without far-reaching effects on trade. In more recent years the Suez crisis of 1956 and the

[6] See *Bull. from Eur. Com.*, April–May, 1963.
[7] Information derived from table in UN, *Economic Developments in the Middle East, 1945 to 1954* (New York, 1955), p. 19.

economic penetration of the Middle East by the Soviet Union and other Eastern European countries have also had adverse effects upon British trade with the Middle East. Nevertheless, the United Kingdom remains one of the leading trade partners of the Middle East.[8]

The major Middle East exporters to the United Kingdom do not enjoy a relationship such as that of the Commonwealth countries, and in all probability they will not be the subject of special arrangements between the United Kingdom and the Common Market when British accession is finally effected. On this basis we must assume that so far as the Middle East is concerned, British membership would present the countries of this area with more or less the same set of questions that they encounter with the present membership of the Common Market. The addition of Britain to the Market will, however, increase the magnitude of Middle East–Common Market problems with respect to certain products.

OIL AND PETROLEUM PRODUCTS

The energy situation in the United Kingdom is basically similar to that in the Common Market countries, which has been discussed earlier.[9] The gap between the production and consumption of energy exists in spite of the fact that the United Kingdom is the largest producer of coal in Western Europe and the third largest in the world. The shortage of coal was attributed in 1956 to the low level of investment in the industry between 1913 and 1947, to the two World Wars, to the greater attraction of less laborious and hazardous industries for miners, and to the steady rise in demand for energy.

In the light of this shortage and its very small hydroelectric po-

[8] Information derived from the tables in UN, *Economic Developments in the Middle East, 1954–1955* (New York, 1956) and *1959–1961* (New York, 1962) at pp. 148–49 and 158–59, respectively.
[9] See Chapter I of this work.

tential, the United Kingdom, like the Common Market countries, has taken steps to produce atomic energy as quickly and abundantly as possible. It is estimated that the coal equivalent of the energy produced will be 5 or 6 million tons in 1965 and 40 million tons in 1975. "Despite this ambitious programme, the contribution of nuclear energy will remain relatively small in the next 20 years and the United Kingdom will be obliged to maintain, and even increase, its output of coal and to make use of substantial quantities of imported petroleum." [10] The United Kingdom is the largest importer, the largest refiner, and the largest consumer of petroleum products in Western Europe.[11]

The four leading oil-exporting countries of the Middle East have furnished the bulk of the United Kingdom's oil imports. In 1961, for example, Iran's exports of crude oil to the United Kingdom amounted to more than $100,000,000 as compared to over $190,-000,000 to all the six Common Market countries combined. Iraq's crude oil exports amounted to more than $120,000,000 as compared to a total of over $412,000,000 to the Common Market. Saudi Arabia's crude oil exports to the United Kingdom were much less in value. They amounted to over $35,000,000, while the Common Market imports amounted to over $260,000,000. But Kuwait's exports of crude oil to the United Kingdom in 1961 were higher in value than its exports to all the Common Market countries combined; they amounted to more than $450,000,000 as compared with over $430,000,000 to the Common Market.[12]

Of the four countries, Kuwait and Iran have been the leading exporters of petroleum products to the United Kingdom. In 1961, for example, Kuwait's exports amounted to over $7,000,000 as compared with over $6,000,000 to the Common Market. Iran's ex-

---

[10] OEEC, *Europe's Growing Needs of Energy, How Can They Be Met?* (Paris, 1956), p. 95.
[11] *Ibid.*, p. 93.   [12] See Tables 4–7.

ports in the same year amounted to over $5,000,000 as compared with over $4,000,000 for all the Common Market countries.[13]

When the United Kingdom becomes a member of the EEC, the Middle East exporters of crude oil will not be adversely affected because the EEC has no common external tariff on crude oil.[14] The impact of British membership may be felt, however, in two other ways. One is the EEC's decision (on the basis of the Treaty of Rome) to levy duties on petroleum products. The application of this tariff by the United Kingdom, if it enters the Market, is bound to affect the Middle East's leading exporters of petroleum products, Kuwait and Iran, unless special arrangements are made to overcome it. In any case, even if the common external tariff is made applicable, its effects cannot be too serious because the Inter-executive Working Party of the EEC, for the present at least, has recommended low duties on petroleum products.[15]

The other way by which Middle East oil exports to the United Kingdom could be affected is through a decrease in British demand by virtue of combining further efforts in the field of atomic energy development with the Common Market countries. Barring a sudden break-through in this field, the probability is that the United Kingdom as well as the present six members of the Community will continue to increase their demands for oil.[16] In general, British accession to the EEC should produce few or no ill effects on Middle East oil exports to the United Kingdom.

CEREALS

Even if the United Kingdom inherits the existing cereal policy of the Common Market upon entry, the Middle East in general will

[13] See Tables 4 and 7.   [14] See List F attached to the Treaty of Rome.
[15] The High Authority of ECSC, the Commission of EEC, and the Commission of Euratom, *Memorandum on Energy Policy* (n.p., June, 1962), pp. 23–24.
[16] See OEEC, *op. cit.*

have little cause for concern. The three major exporters of cereals (barley, wheat, and rice) to the Common Market are Iraq, Syria, and Egypt. Syria's exports of wheat and Egypt's exports of rice to the United Kingdom are nil or negligible. But Iraq's barley exports to Britain are of some significance. In 1952 Iraq's barley exports to the Kingdom amounted to over $20,000,000 as compared with over $5,000,000 to the Common Market countries as a whole. Although these exports dropped enormously in succeeding years, the United Kingdom is still a major market for Iraqi barley. It is interesting to note that the drop in Iraqi barley exports to the United Kingdom has been paralleled by an increase in exports to the Market countries. In 1956, for example, exports to the United Kingdom dropped to around $1,000,000 as compared with over $9,000,000 to the Common Market countries.[17] Thus the British accession will hardly produce any significantly adverse effect on the Middle East exports of wheat, barley, and rice.

VEGETABLES AND FRUITS

The major Middle East exporters of vegetables to the Common Market are Egypt and Lebanon, but only the former is a major exporter to the United Kingdom. In 1952, for example, Egypt's exports to Britain amounted to over $3,000,000, while those to the six Common Market countries were over $1,500,000. By 1956, however, exports to the Common Market countries had increased over those to the United Kingdom. Nevertheless, Egypt is still the Middle East's leading vegetable exporter to the United Kingdom.

Almost all the Middle East exporters of fresh fruits to the Common Market export also to Britain. The two leading exporters, however, are Israel and Turkey. Israeli exports of fresh fruits to the United Kingdom are of particular significance. In 1952 they

[17] See Table 23.

were worth more than $12,000,000, and in 1956 nearly $18,500,-000. In the latter year the total value of Israel's fresh fruit exports was $38,000,000.[18] In that same year Common Market countries imported a total of about $10,000,000. In spite of the fact that exports of Israeli fresh fruits to the EEC countries have increased enormously, the United Kingdom is still the largest market for Israel in Western Europe. Should the Common Market duties in the transitional period and eventually the common external tariff on citrus fruits become applicable to Israeli exports to the United Kingdom, Israel will probably suffer seriously.

The two major exporters of dried fruits to the Common Market also export substantial amounts to the United Kingdom. Turkey, however, leads. In 1956 Turkish exports to the United Kingdom amounted to nearly $4,000,000, as compared to over $7,000,000 for all the Common Market countries combined.[19] The application of the Common Market duties to Turkish exports of dried fruits to the United Kingdom will obviously produce serious difficulties for Turkey.

OTHER MAJOR EXPORTS TO THE UNITED KINGDOM

All the four leading exporters of Middle East cotton also export to the United Kingdom. These are Egypt, Iran, Syria, and Turkey. Egypt is the leading exporter to the United Kingdom. Although the value of Egypt's cotton exports to the United Kingdom, as well as those of the other Middle East countries, is far below that of its exports to the Common Market, it should be stressed that the United Kingdom's markets are of particular importance to these countries. Egypt's exports in 1954 amounted to over $35,000,000, though they dropped to about $8,000,000 in 1956. On the other hand, Iran's cotton exports to the United Kingdom increased during the same period. They rose from about

[18] *Ibid.*　　　　　　　[19] *Ibid.*

$1,500,000 to over $3,000,000. In any event, since there is no common external tariff on cotton, membership of the United Kingdom would probably have no significant ill effect on the cotton exports of the Middle East.

Turkey, which is the Middle East's only important exporter of tobacco to the Common Market, is also the area's leading exporter to the United Kingdom. As compared with the six Common Market countries, the value of the Turkish tobacco exported to the United Kingdom would seem small. In 1956, for example, Turkish exports to the United Kingdom amounted to over $2,000,000, while those to the Common Market countries amounted to over $19,000,000. In that year Turkish exports to its chief customer in the Common Market area, Germany, were worth more than four times as much as its exports to the United Kingdom. Thus, even if the duty-free quota arrangement for tobacco between the EEC and Turkey is not applied to Turkish exports to the United Kingdom, the exports are not large enough to hurt the interests of Turkey seriously. In all probability, however, the United Kingdom will treat Turkish tobacco exports in the same way that the Common Market does.

The last major export item of the Middle East to the United Kingdom is carpets and rugs. Iran is the leading exporter of rugs to the United Kingdom, as it is to the Common Market. In 1952 Iranian carpets going to the United Kingdom were worth more than $2,000,000; but this increased to nearly $3,000,000 in 1954 and to over $4,500,000 in 1956. In the last year the exports to the United Kingdom were about half the value of the exports to all the Common Market countries combined. Iranian rug exports to both the United Kingdom and the Common Market countries have increased in recent years. Should the arrangement between the Common Market and Iran mentioned earlier become applicable to the exports of Persian rugs to the United Kingdom, Iran will probably not be unhappy.

PART II

Middle East Attitudes and Policies toward the European Common Market

VI

Attempts at Cooperation in the Non-Arab Countries of the Middle East

IN THE first part of this study the broad impact of the Common Market on the exports of the Middle East was examined in terms of its already discernible effects and with a view to its potential implications in the light of progressive implementation of the Treaty of Rome as well as the association of Greece and African states and even the possibility of Britain's membership in the European Economic Community. Although the emerging oil policy of the EEC, its regulations and policies in the grain, vegetable, and fruit sectors, or even its cotton policy may in future pose significant challenges to the exports of the Arab countries of the Middle East, the fact remains that up to the present time the most serious effects of the Common Market have been felt by the non-Arab countries of the Middle East—Iran, Israel, and Turkey.

Yet these are the very countries that have reacted most favorably to the establishment of the Common Market. Although they have been keenly aware of the ill effects of the EEC on their exports and on their over-all economies, they have persistently sought to reconcile their interests with those of the Common Market. A cynic might remark that their economic dependence on the EEC has left them no other choice, but detailed examination would reveal that other considerations, of a political, ideological, geographic, historical, and psychological nature, have inclined them not to look for other choices. In the following pages the influence of some of these considerations on the policies of the three non-Arab countries of the Middle East toward the EEC will be analyzed.

ISRAEL'S REACTION

Of the three non-Arab countries, Israel reacted most promptly to the formation of the Common Market. An Israeli delegation to the Common Market was accredited as early as January 30, 1959. Israel was the third country, after the United States and Greece, to establish a diplomatic mission at the EEC headquarters in Brussels. The considerations underlying Israel's swift action are varied. The most important has been the impact of the Common Market on Israeli exports. As was seen earlier, Israel has traditionally exported large quantities of its products to the Common Market countries. The European markets have proved most beneficial to Israeli exports for a number of reasons. The country's geographic proximity to Europe and the cheap transportation by way of the Mediterranean Sea have played an important role. At present no other market would seem to be as advantageous for Israel. The Afro-Asian countries could hardly provide Israel with as lucrative a market as that of Europe. In part this is because of similar climatic and natural conditions. The demand for Israeli citrus fruits in African and Asian markets is not great. The demand for other major Israeli exports is also negligible in these countries. Diamonds, textiles, and machinery, for example, are so expensive that their markets are largely limited to the highly industrialized countries of Western Europe.

Another important consideration motivating Israel in its reaction to the Common Market is the possibility of British accession. The United Kingdom is the largest single market for Israeli fresh fruits in Western Europe.[1] If Britain should enter the Common Market, the ill effects of the Market on Israeli citrus fruit exports would increase; almost 45 per cent of the Israeli exports are directed to Britain and the EEC.[2] If the United Kingdom should remain outside the Market, this fact could prove beneficial, in case Israel fails to reach some kind of accommodation with the EEC, to the extent that Britain could absorb additional Israeli citrus fruits.

Closely related to these two considerations underlying the Israeli position vis-à-vis the Common Market is the desire to maintain high standards of living. Israel believes that a continuation of the adverse effects of the Common Market on the exports of its products would eventually result in a substantial reduction in the standards of living of its people. Michael Tsur, Director-General of the Israeli Ministry of Commerce and Industry, thinks that the present situation serves to weaken Israeli competitive ability and keep the standards of living "lower than in any other country of modern industrial development." [3]

A fourth consideration influencing the Israeli reaction to the Common Market involves the Arab economic boycott. Ever since the Armistice Agreements of 1949 between Israel and the Arab neighboring countries, the Arabs have maintained a total economic boycott against Israel. The Arab countries have taken the position that a state of war continues to exist. Hence Egypt has refused to allow Israeli ships and cargoes through the otherwise easily accessible Suez Canal. This situation has tended to isolate Israel in the Middle East. To the extent that the Common Market tends to cut off Israel from Europe it would serve, the Israelis believe,

[1] For details see Chapter V and Table 23.
[2] *New York Times*, April 19, 1963, p. 57.
[3] "Israel and European Common Market," *Israel Economic Forum*, December, 1962, p. 16.

"unintentionally and indirectly as a tool in aid of the Arab boycott." [4]

A fifth consideration cited in support of Israel's desire to have some kind of an arrangement with the EEC is the country's "fundamental" ties with Europe. Israel has stressed its historical, cultural, and social ties with the European people. It has also pointed to its basic community of interest with the West in political matters. Pinhas Sapir, Israeli Minister of Commerce and Industry, stated on February 11, 1962, that the Mediterranean is not a frontier of Europe; it is a bridge. "Israel is not only a country geographically situated at a corner of this bridge," he continued, "our ties with Europe are fundamental. Our way of life, our cultural and social orientation makes us a part of Europe. These factors are as much a reason for our desire to take part in European economic developments as economic considerations." [5]

In the light of these considerations the government of Israel made its earliest overtures to the Common Market soon after the establishment of its delegation at the EEC headquarters at Brussels. These were politely repulsed on the ground that the EEC was at the time engaged in detailed negotiations with the government of Greece. Subsequent to the EEC-Greek Agreement, Israel again pressed for some form of an arrangement—perhaps one similar to that between Greece and the Common Market. But apparently terms similar to those of the Athens Agreement were not obtainable at the time. During the early part of February, 1962, an eighteen-member delegation from the Parliamentary Assembly of the EEC visited Israel. Following their reports to the EEC, in May, 1962, the Israeli delegation, headed by Ambassador Amiel Najar,

---

[4] *Ibid.*

[5] See *Israel Digest of Press and Events in Israel and the Middle East*, March 2, 1962. For an exposition of the same theme, see Moshe Bartur, Israeli Ambassador and Permanent Delegate to the European Office of the United Nations, "Israel and the Economic Integration of Europe," *Israel Export and Trade Journal*, December, 1960, p. 13.

conducted talks with the EEC experts, headed by Philipp Masserer of Germany. In July of the same year the Council of Ministers received the recommendation of the EEC Commission for the opening of negotiations with Israel.

Eventually negotiations were opened on November 26, 1962, in Brussels between a Community delegation under the chairmanship of Gunter Seeliger, Director-General of External Relations in the Commission, and an Israeli government delegation. The aim of these negotiations was to find some form of agreement or other arrangement in the commercial field between the EEC and Israel.[6]

The Israeli efforts have not been confined to diplomatic channels alone. Israel has launched a campaign aimed at obtaining support for its proposals within the Common Market area. Special information programs have been sent to EEC member countries, and various groups have been invited to visit Israel. These efforts have not been without effect in creating an atmosphere favorable to the successful conduct of negotiations between Israel and the EEC. For example, the Liberal International, which met in Tel Aviv in January, 1963, urged European liberals to press in Common Market countries for the removal of trade barriers erected against specifically affected countries such as Israel. In a keynote address to the convention, Professor Giovanni Malagochi, president of the Italian Liberal party, stated that the EEC must be expanded to include Israel. A pledge of support for the Israeli position in negotiations with the EEC has also been made by other groups such as the European Trade Union Secretariat.[7]

In addition to its diplomatic efforts and campaigns for securing the support of various groups in the EEC area, Israel has sought to impress upon the Common Market countries the degree of its determination to cooperate with the Community by resorting to far-reaching reforms in its economy. On February 9, 1962, Levi

---

[6] *Bulletin of the European Economic Community*, January, 1963, p. 27.
[7] See *Israel Digest of Press*, November 23, 1962.

Eshkol, Israel's Minister of Finance, announced the inauguration of Israel's New Economic Policy (NEP). The basic purpose of the NEP is to make Israeli products more competitive abroad and thereby to ease her association or agreement with the EEC. The primary means adopted to attain this end are currency devaluation, the abolition of multiple exchange rates, and the reduction of numerous tariffs and of subsidies and premiums. All these reforms aim at adapting the economic conditions in Israel to the requirements of the Common Market for some kind of association in the future. As a matter of policy the Common Market has taken the position that its Agreement of Association with Greece cannot become a universal model for the association of other countries because conditions differ from one country to another.[8] Having failed to reach a full association agreement with the EEC, Israel has sought to obtain tariff and quota concessions on nearly forty groups of items, including oranges. It has also demanded duty-free entry into the Market for goods processed in Israel but made from raw materials originally purchased from the Community. At the present time negotiations between the EEC and Israel are at a standstill because the Israeli demands had to be referred back to the Community's Council of Ministers.[9]

IRAN'S REACTION

The reaction of Iran to the Common Market manifested itself later than did that of Israel, but ever since March, 1962, the government of Iran has been seriously interested in the development of the Common Market as it affects the interests of Iran. The basic considerations underlying the position of Iran vis-à-vis the Common Market are varied. The most important is the impact of the

[8] See EEC Commission, *The First Stage of the Common Market: Report on the Execution of the Treaty (January 1958—January 1962)* (Brussels, 1962), p. 99.
[9] *European Community*, September, 1963, p. 5.

EEC on Iranian exports. Iran's most important exports to the Common Market have traditionally been dried fruits and carpets, but, as has been seen earlier, these are by no means the only exports. Iran's first reaction to the Common Market followed the successful Greek association. The Iranian government was alarmed by this development because the preferred position of Greek dried fruits would adversely affect the exportation of Iranian dried fruits to the Common Market. Furthermore, Iran, like Israel and most other Middle East countries, depends significantly on its exports to the United Kingdom. The possibility of British accession to the EEC alarmed Iran and spurred its efforts to find some kind of a solution to the problems created by the Common Market. Alienation of the Common Market and the markets in the United Kingdom is feared by Iran, not only because it must export to these traditional markets in order to live, but also because Iran wishes to avoid any difficulty that might force expansion of its trade with its northern neighbor, the Soviet Union. Although trade with Russia is considerable, Iran's pre-1939 dependence on Russian markets is remembered with bitterness. This dependence had for many decades opened Iran's northern provinces to the unrivaled political influence of Russia. The memory of this unhappy experience has led Iran to guard against excessive dependence upon the easily accessible Russian markets.

Closely related to this cautious trade policy toward the Soviet Union is Iran's current policy of "positive nationalism," which favors close economic and political ties with the West as manifested in the country's membership in the Western-sponsored military alliance of the Central Treaty Organization (CENTO) and in its defense pact with the United States. Thus for both economic and political reasons Iran has sought to reach some kind of an arrangement with the Common Market.

Iran's first move toward that end took place during the government of Dr. Amini. The former Prime Minister toured the capitals of Belgium, West Germany, and France in March, 1962, discussing Iran's predicament with the officials of the EEC and some of the member states. Dr. Amini had also expressed interest in seeking the assistance of the Common Market in Iran's third Seven-Year Plan for economic development.[10] On July 24, 1962, the EEC Council of Ministers instructed the Commission to start exploratory negotiations with Iran. The Iranian government subsequently stepped up its study of the problems raised by the Common Market and dispatched its first mission to the Common Market for negotiations in October, 1962. During his four-day visit to Brussels, Dr. Jahanshahi, the Iranian Minister of Commerce, explored with Walter Hallstein, the President of the EEC Commission, the "mutual interests" of Iran and the Common Market. From Iranian press reports it was evident that Iran's success in negotiations had not been ensured and that Iran had hinted at "counter measures" in case the Common Market proved impervious to its demands.[11] This position became even more evident when it was reported that the Iranian Regulatory Commission on Exports and Imports was considering the possibility of placing limitations on imports from the EEC if the Common Market should continue its "harmful" policy.[12]

The second stage of Iran's negotiations with the Common Market began on October 1, 1962. The Iranian Mission, headed by Dr. Alikhani, the Minister of Commerce, and the staff of the Commission held talks on ways and means of improving and expanding trade between the Six and Iran, as requested by Iran in a memorandum of May 24, 1962. At the time it was envisaged that a report on these talks would be submitted to the Council, which would decide whether or not to open negotiations for the conclusion of a trade agreement between the EEC, its Member States, and Iran.[13]

[10] See Ettela't Havai, No. 3700.   [11] Ibid., No. 3873.   [12] Ibid., No. 3874.
[13] Cf. Bull. of EEC, December, 1962, p. 17, and Ettela't Havai, Nos. 4030, 4036, 4042, and 4044.

Such an agreement would plainly fall far short of the association agreement that Iran might have wished to conclude at the earliest stage of its talks with the EEC officials. But apparently Iran has found a trade agreement compatible with its interests at the present time.

Upon his return to Tehran from Brussels Dr. Alikhani termed his talks with the Common Market officials "successful." [14] Later, however, he stated that the results of the negotiations were "relatively satisfactory" and expressed the hope that within a month or two an agreement would be signed. "The most important problem" pertained to exports of Iranian raisins, the tariff for which was reduced, as a result of negotiations, from 8 per cent to 1 per cent. Furthermore, it was agreed that out of a total of 14,000 tons of raisins exported to the Common Market about 4,000 tons might enter the EEC area without any duties. In regard to carpets, the Iranian delegation had argued that more than 50 per cent of Iran's carpets are manufactured by peasants whose economic future was of particular concern to Iran. The EEC had proposed that the tariff on carpets should be 32 per cent ad valorem up to a certain price; above that price it should be $5 per square meter. Iran was inclined to accept the $5 duty per square meter because its carpets are high-priced carpets. The duties on dried apricots were increased from 7 per cent to 8 per cent, but Iran was satisfied because of the absence of competitors. The duties on caviar, another major export, were reduced from 30 per cent to 24 per cent, to the satisfaction of Iran.[15]

On September 25, 1963, the EEC and Iran initialed a trade agreement to take effect on January 1, 1964. This agreement is the first of its kind between the EEC and a third country under Article 111 of the Treaty of Rome. It does not envisage a customs union. Rather, it provides for temporary, nondiscriminatory reductions of

[14] See *Ettela't Havai*, No. 4050.   [15] *Ibid.*, No. 4054.

the common external tariff and tariff quotas on exports of particular importance to Iran, such as carpets, caviar, and dried grapes and apricots.[16]

TURKEY'S REACTION

The third non-Arab country of the Middle East which has sought to cooperate with the Common Market is Turkey. The Turkish application from the very outset aimed at association with the EEC. Unlike Israel and Iran, Turkey is regarded by the Common Market countries as a logical applicant for association not only because of its geographic position, but also because Turkey is already a member of some European organizations such as NATO and OECD. Turkey requested association with the Common Market on July 31, 1959, a month or so after the Greek application was made. The Turkish application was favorably endorsed by the EEC Council of Ministers on September 11, 1959, and negotiations to ward an association agreement were in progress without interruption until the military coup in 1960.[17]

The first meeting between the Turkish delegation and the representatives of the Common Market Commission took place in September, 1959. At the end of the discussions a communiqué was issued in which the substance of the talks was included. The parties discussed the problems raised by the application of Turkey for association; the Community expressed a hope that it might be able to give Turkey financial assistance; the possibility of a customs union was explored; and harmonization of Turkey's trade policy with that of the EEC was considered.[18] Further talks were planned, but the coup in Turkey postponed these.

The new Turkish regime resumed negotiations in October, 1960.

---

[16] *Ibid.*, Nos. 4174 and 4175. See also *Eur. Com.*, October, 1963, p. 2.
[17] See *Bulletin from the European Community*, December, 1960, p. 16.
[18] See *ibid.*, October–November, 1959, pp. 4–5.

The ten-man Turkish delegation for these talks was headed by Dr. Cihat Iren, the former Turkish Minister of Commerce. On March 21, 1961, the Council of Ministers of the Common Market discussed the Turkish application, and on April 10 the Turkish government continued negotiations with the EEC Commission.[19] At various intervals during 1962 the negotiations were continued, and the Council of Ministers discussed how an association agreement with Turkey should be drafted and what it should contain. These questions were also discussed during the early part of 1963.[20] The four years of protracted negotiations were indicative of the special problems that Turkish association would pose.

Turkey is beset with profound economic and political problems. In the postwar period a huge military establishment has been superimposed upon a basically underdeveloped economy. The American emphasis on military alliances, even in areas where the economy is poor, has tended to nullify the benefits that might be derived from economic assistance. This has partly been the case in Turkey. In spite of the fact that the new regime has committed itself to "rapid economic progress within a regime of freedom," as late as February, 1963, the situation in Turkey was characterized in these terms: "The billions of dollars that the West has poured into Turkey in the last fifteen years have been largely misspent, in the sense that no real economic progress has been made. By now most people appreciate the absurdity of a country, in which the income per head still stands at about 58 pounds per annum, maintaining an army larger than those of the richest nations of Western Europe." [21]

It is now also clear that the armed forces revolution of May, 1960, which interrupted the Turkish-EEC negotiations, has not necessarily produced a politically stable Turkey. The mass purge of more

[19] See *ibid.*, April, 1961, p. 2.

[20] See *Bull. of EEC*, December, 1962, p. 17, January, 1963, p. 27, and February, 1963, p. 34.

[21] See *The Economist*, February 9, 1963, p. 498.

than 7,000 army officers shortly after the revolution resulted in a large number of disgruntled men, who supported the abortive coup of the war college cadets in May, 1963. The shooting that erupted between the cadets and the new Turkish regime was a reminder of the basic political instability of Turkey in spite of Premier Ismet Inönü's assurances that "constitutional order and democratic regime will forever live in Turkey with honor." [22]

While these conditions of economic underdevelopment and political instability have made the problem of Turkish association with EEC more acute, the fact that these conditions exist on the southern flank of NATO has demanded the inclusion of Turkey within the prospering economy of the Community. Turkey is not only an important strategic ally of the Common Market countries but also a major economic partner. At present 30 per cent of Turkey's exports go to the Community, and 35 per cent of its imports come from the six member nations. The conclusive association of Turkey will add 25 million people to the population of the Community, which is about 220 million without 8 million Greeks and over 50 million inhabitants of African associates.

The first major step toward definitive association of Turkey with the Common Market was taken shortly after the problem of financial assistance to Turkey was settled.[23] On June 25, 1963, representatives of the government of Turkey and of the Common Market Commission initialed a draft association agreement. This draft is to be presented for approval to the Community's Council of Ministers, which must make its decision by unanimous vote after consulting the European Parliament. It will then be submitted for

[22] *New York Times*, May 22, 1963. Political instability in Turkey was also in evidence in August, 1963, when possibly 200 people were arrested in Ankara, Istanbul, and other parts of Turkey. Most of the arrested seemed to be politicians, writers, teachers, journalists, and other intellectuals. The Turkish authorities indicated unofficially that those arrested were "leftists and Communists." See *New York Times*, August 19, 1963.

[23] See Conseils des Communautés Européenes, Secrétariat Général, *Communication à la Presse* (Brussels, April 2, 1963), p. 12.

ratification by the parliaments of the member states and of Turkey.

The draft agreement envisages a customs union between Turkey and the Common Market with the aim of integrating Turkey with the Community in an association framework but with the possibility of Turkish application for full membership in the distant future. Turkish economic problems have clearly prompted the parties to the agreement to favor a cautious, gradual, and flexible approach to eventual Turkish association. This objective is to be reached in three distinct and successive stages: preparatory, transitional, and definitive. The preparatory phase, which is planned to last five years, will be used to help Turkey "put its economy on a sound footing" before the establishment of a customs union with the Common Market. The aid will be given by the Common Market in two major forms: trade preferences and financial assistance. Trade preferences in the Community will apply to roughly 37 per cent of Turkish exports, including tobacco and some dried fruits. The financial assistance up to a maximum of $175,000,000 will be granted through the European Investment Bank in the form of loans for investment projects forming part of the Turkish development plan.

The customs union will be introduced gradually during the transitional period, which is expected to last twelve years. Although detailed arrangements for this period were not set down, the main outlines were sketched. Among these was the provision that the customs union will cover trade in all commodities, with Turkey adopting the Common Market's common external tariff. Turkey will also align its economic policy with that of the European Economic Community.

The last definitive phase will be based on the customs union introduced in the transitional period, but it will also involve increasingly close coordination of the economies of Turkey and the EEC.[24]

[24] *European Community*, July–August, 1963, pp. 10–11.

It may be asked whether the association of Turkey with the Common Market in Europe will adversely affect the possibility of the establishment of a common market between Iran, Turkey, and Pakistan, the regional members of the Central Treaty Organization.[25] Although this organization was created initially for the purpose of defense and in the past has placed its greatest emphasis on military cooperation between its member states, it is now more than ever before concerned with economic cooperation among its members. This change of emphasis has come about in part as a result of the changing attitude of the United States which has been in evidence since the late 1950's, particularly since President Kennedy took office. It is now realized that the former American attempts to balloon the military strength of basically underdeveloped countries like Iran, Turkey, and Pakistan may well prove ineffective in the absence of socioeconomic and political development in these societies. This realization has coincided with the growing concern of the regional members of CENTO with the European Common Market. In July, 1962, when the Turkish Mission, headed by the Turkish Foreign Minister, visited Iran for a series of talks in regard to the expansion of Turko-Iranian ties, the question of an Irano-Turko-Pakistani common market was considered.[26]

It is believed that over-all economic cooperation of the regional members of CENTO in the past has paved the way toward the eventual creation of such a common market. In fact, this cooperation has extended beyond the exclusively economic sphere, embracing activities essential for the expansion of trade and economic development. Both the United States and Great Britain have given assistance to the road and railway systems of the regional members as evidenced by their aid for the Karachi-Tchah-Bahar Road and for the linking up of the Turkish and Iranian railways via Ghatar and Khoy. The two Western countries have also furthered regional

[25] Great Britain is the only non-Middle Eastern member of CENTO. The United States belongs to some of its committees.

[26] See *Ettela't Havai*, No. 3812.

telecommunications as, for example, the Ankara-Tehran-Karachi microwave system and the project for the improvement of the existing high-frequency radiotelephone and radiotelegraph circuits connecting the regional capitals with London.

In addition to these improvements in transportation and communication, other measures have been undertaken to assist the establishment of a common market between the three countries. Agriculture, of course, is the backbone of their economy. Therefore cooperation has taken place in pest control, the improvement of animal breeding methods, and forest conservation. Simultaneously a center for training and research in animal production and artificial insemination and one for training in the use and repair of agricultural machinery have been established in Karachi and in Tehran, respectively. Furthermore, a multilateral fund has been created for increasing technical cooperation.[27]

With regard to trade between the regional member countries as well as with third countries, the Economic Committee of CENTO has sought ways of marketing common products, standardizing agricultural products, easing the flow of transit trade through the regional countries, unifying and simplifying customs formalities, and facilitating the travel and residence of businessmen and tourists by abolishing visa fees and granting visas with a minimum of formality for longer periods of time. There is hope that these objectives will be vigorously pursued in the future now that the CENTO Council of Ministers in their eleventh session held at Karachi in late April and early May, 1963, have decided to place far greater emphasis upon the economic activities of CENTO. In the official communiqué issued at the end of the session it was stated that the completion of port facilities at Trebizond has already increased commercial exchanges among the member countries.[28]

Should these developments be accelerated and political circum-

---

[27] For further information, see, for example, *Free World Forum*, Vol. 2, No. 4, and CENTO, *Five Years of CENTO* (Ankara, n.d.).

[28] For the text of this communiqué, see *Ettela't Havai*, No. 4039.

stances continue to favor the existing relationship among the three regional members, CENTO could probably provide the framework for some kind of common market between Iran, Turkey, and Pakistan. Turkish association with the European Common Market is not expected to affect adversely the emergence of a common market for Turkey and the other two Muslim countries. In the same way that Turkey is simultaneously a member of NATO and CENTO, it could also be an associate member of the European Common Market and a full member of an Irano-Turko-Pakistani common market.

VII

The Signs of Opposition
The Arab Countries of the Middle East

THE Arab countries of the Middle East, as has been seen, have suffered less than the non-Arab countries from the establishment of the Common Market, although there is no reason to minimize the potential future challenge of the EEC to their exports. Barley, wheat, rice, vegetables, and fresh fruits may well suffer progressively from implementation of the Treaty of Rome as well as from preferential treatment accorded to exports of African associates or as the result of other developments which have already been discussed. Even exports of Arab oil might suffer if Algerian oil should enter the Common Market on a preferential basis and if Algeria should become an economic competitor rather than a political ally of the Arab Middle East. Nevertheless, Arab exports in general have not been so hard hit as those of the non-Arab countries.

Yet the Arab countries have been the ones which, in general, have expressed serious opposition to the Common Market. This attitude cannot be attributed to Arab assessments of the actual or potential effects of the EEC on their economies. In fact, no reasoned and systematic study, to the best of our knowledge, exists of the impact of the Common Market on the exports of the Arab countries. Apart from isolated and unsubstantiated statements in the Arab press or by some Arab statesmen about the "dangers" of the Common Market, one will search in vain for serious studies on this subject. But there is an abundance of materials on which to draw for explaining the factors underlying Arab opposition to the Common Market.

The reasons are by no means simple or neatly separated. On the contrary, they are complex and interrelated. In fact, the problem is often compounded by the difficulty of distinguishing between serious statements of policy and propagandistic vituperations. Nevertheless, an attempt will be made in the following pages to analyze the major considerations shaping the Arab attitude toward the Common Market.

Parenthetically, the reader is reminded that we shall use the term "Arab" in a collective sense referring to the Arab countries included in this study, although the dominant tone of the Arab attitude toward the Common Market is most often set by Egypt. However, an attempt will be made to indicate, insofar as it is compatible with the scope of this study, significant variations in Arab feelings about the EEC. The basic factors underlying the opposition relate to the Arab-Israeli conflict, "Arab" ambitions in Africa, and the East-West struggle.

FEAR OF CLOSE RELATIONS BETWEEN ISRAEL AND THE COMMON MARKET

Underlying the Arab attitude toward the Common Market is fear of a close relationship between Israel and the EEC, particularly of a relationship that takes the form of associate membership or "any other form that should materially benefit Israel." The Arab fear is basically related to the determination of the Arab countries to maintain the boycott of Israel by every possible means. They seem to believe that this boycott may be neutralized in two ways: through close economic ties between Israel and the Common Market and through the salutary effects of such ties on the economic activities of Israel in Africa.

The Common Market countries are at present Israel's most important market, and the total or partial loss of this market would be regarded by some Israeli observers as "disastrous." Some even regard the whole Common Market problem as a "matter of life and death" for Israel.[1] To the Arabs an Israeli failure to reach agreement with the EEC would be a cause for rejoicing. They believe that if Israel should achieve an agreement that protected its interests and enhanced its economic position, the Arab boycott would be seriously weakened. When the possibility of Israeli "membership" was rumored, Al Ahram commented that the Israeli effort was "intended to weaken the Arab boycott which led to this critical situation [that is, the Israeli economic difficulties]. Thus the preservation of Israel seems to be regarded as more important than the limiting and weakening of its industrial growth, which is an inevitable consequence of its membership in the Market."[2]

Critical of the Common Market for the same reason, Al Anwar stated: "The entry of Israel into the Market will enhance its aggressive attitude and will help it to find a way out of its economic crisis. As far as the Arabs are concerned, it will affect the Arab boycott." With a hint of countermeasures against the Common Market, the Lebanese paper stated, "This will prompt the Arabs to reconsider their position toward many countries with which they have broad economic dealings."[3]

It is also feared that an agreement between Israel and the Com-

[1] Moshe Allon, head of the economics section of the Israeli Foreign Ministry, has been quoted as saying, "The Common Market will destroy our economy if no arrangement is found with it" (New York Times, February 6, 1962).
[2] Al Ahram, March 5, 1962.   [3] Al Anwar, March 6, 1962.

mon Market may weaken the Arab boycott by reinforcing Israeli economic activities in Africa. The motives of Israel in pursuing a vigorous economic policy in Africa are varied. When the Israeli Foreign Minister, Mrs. Golda Meir, was questioned about them during her second tour of Africa, she stated, "Israel wants something in return for the cooperation and goodwill it brings to African peoples and governments. This great thing is friendship." [4] Befriending the Africans is not, however, incompatible with Israel's desire to overcome the dire effects of the Arab boycott. Israel's policy has aimed at overstepping the Arab boycott and "establishing good relations with her neighbours' neighbours." [5]

These good relations cover a wide variety of fields and are not confined to the diplomatic sphere; since the fall of 1962 Israel has succeeded in establishing relations with twenty-one African states. [6] The fundamental reason for the success of Israel in Africa is perhaps the fact that it possesses skills and experience that the Africans need and want. The technical skills of small and developing Israel are more appropriate to the African states than those of large and developed countries like the United States or the Soviet Union. [7] Whatever else may explain the attraction of Israel for the Africans, the fact is that Israel has managed, in spite of the adverse propaganda of Egypt and the Soviet Union, to build up an important role for itself in the modernization of Africa.

Israeli technical assistance, for example, has helped the Africans, not only in city planning, union organization, and the like, but also in the all-important field of agriculture. By the fall of 1962 Israel had about a thousand technicians in more than thirty-five countries and territories of Africa. But Israeli efforts have extended far beyond technical assistance. The African states have received Is-

---

[4] *Midstream*, Spring, 1961, p. 12.

[5] *World Today*, January, 1958, pp. 38–40.

[6] *Washington Post*, September 25, 1962.

[7] See Michael Brecher, "Israel and 'Afro-Asia,' " *International Journal*, Spring, 1961, p. 128.

raeli instructors and have sent students to Israel. By the fall of 1962 there were a thousand African students in Israel studying various subjects, particularly those of interest to modernizing nations. Special international seminars have been conducted for Africans, some under the auspices of the Afro-Asian Institute for Labour Studies and Cooperation.[8]

The Arab states have adopted several different courses of action in order to bar an Israeli agreement with the Common Market. First of all, they have kept close watch on contacts between the Common Market and Israel. The Arab press has rather consistently followed the Israeli–Common Market negotiations, has reported the exchange of visits between Israeli and Common Market officials, and has rejoiced over the news that associate membership is not at present open to Israel.[9]

More important, the Arab states have individually or collectively sought to bring pressure upon the Common Market against an agreement favorable to Israel. The leading Arab antagonist has been Egypt. The government of the United Arab Republic expressed its "grave concern" to West Germany when the Ludwig Erhard–Levi Eshkol talks were taking place. The Foreign Ministry of the UAR declared that "Israeli membership in the Market is considered an act of aggression against the security of the Arab States." [10] The other Arab states have also sought, through bilateral contacts, to bring pressure upon the Market. "These contacts were intended to convince the Common Market members not to accept the Israeli membership; moreover, the Arab states threatened to boycott the Market should Israel join it." [11] The same source hailed the news of obstacle to Israeli "membership" by stating, "The Lebanese Foreign Ministry received heartening news on the position

[8] Israel Office of Information, "The Afro-Asian Institute for Labour Studies and Cooperation in Israel," June 16, 1960.

[9] See, for example, *Akher Sa'a*, February 7, 1962, and *Al Ahram*, January 24, 1962, and March 4, 1962.

[10] *Al Gomhouriya*, March 7, 1962.   [11] *Beirut al-Masa*, March 11, 1962.

of the member states in the EEC vis-à-vis the Israeli application for membership. The news is that the EEC will not endorse the Israeli application, at least at the present time, on the ground that Israel is not in Europe." [12]

The Arab states have also collectively opposed the Common Market because of its relationship with Israel. The main vehicle for the expression of their collective opposition has been the Arab League. The General Secretary of the League pressed the Ambassador of West Germany in Cairo for clarification of the German position regarding the efforts of Israel,[13] and the Secretariat of the League sent a memorandum to Common Market officials stating that if Israel were accepted in the European Market the "prospective Arab Common Market will have to boycott the European Common Market. It will also cooperate with other international markets regardless of their nationalities." [14]

The Arab Economic Council of the League in its meeting of May 30, 1962, resolved:

To notify the member states of the European Common Market that the Arab states—in case of Israeli association with EEC or in case any assistance is given to Israel in any way whereby it may take advantage of the Agreement [the Treaty of Rome]—will reconsider the structure of their foreign trade with the member states of EEC as well as the petroleum policy toward the same group. The Arab states will not allow their own resources to be used to bolster the Israeli economy;

To request the diplomatic missions of the Arab states to EEC members to explore the possible means of exerting pressure on the governments of these states with the object of thwarting Israeli association with EEC and of preventing any advantages that may accrue to Israel from the Treaty [of Rome] in accordance with the decision of the Arab League Council of April 3, 1962;

To lay a plan to establish closer relations between the Arab states and

[12] Ibid. [13] Al Ahram, March 5, 1962.
[14] Beirut al-Masa, March 11, 1962.

the African countries, which are a primary field in the future economic struggle between the Arab states and Israel. The measures that could be taken in this regard would be organized financial, technical, and educational aid to the African states, whether by individual Arab states or by the League.[15]

THE AFRICAN CIRCLE

The Arab attitude toward the Common Market, however, has not been motivated merely by hostility toward Israel and fear that an Israeli agreement with the Common Market might nullify their boycott. The United Arab Republic, in particular, is opposed to the Common Market for other reasons also. One of these is President Nasser's well-known ambition to guide the Pan-African movement. In his book, *Egypt's Liberation*, he makes no secret of Egypt's interests in Africa, which he designates as the "second circle." In too confident a tone he writes that "the peoples of Africa will continue to look to us, who guard their northern gate, and who constitute their link with the outside world." As to Africa, he states, "I may say without exaggeration that we cannot, under any circumstances, however much we might desire it, remain aloof from the terrible and sanguinary conflict going on there today between five million whites and 200 million Africans. We cannot do so for an important and obvious reason: we are in Africa." "We will never in any circumstances," he writes, "be able to relinquish our responsibility to support, with all our might, the spread of enlightenment and civilization to the remotest depths of the jungle." [16]

When President Nasser entertained these hopes, there was no European Common Market, but African nationalism was apparent

<hr/>

[15] See Isma'il Muhammad Khalil (ed.), *Tajribat al-Suq al-Urubbiyah al-Mushtarakah* (Cairo, n.d.), pp. 165–67.

[16] Washington, 1955, pp. 109–10.

everywhere, and Egypt wished to champion it. The establishment of the Common Market hampered Egyptian ambitions somewhat because it provided a basis of cooperation between many African countries and six European states. Part Four of the Treaty of Rome provided for the association of "these countries and territories" with the Common Market.[17] Seventeen of these countries and territories are today African states.[18] A convention has implemented the relevant provisions of the Treaty of Rome governing their relationship with the six European countries for the past five years and is presently to be replaced by a new convention.[19]

The association of the seventeen African states with EEC in effect deprived President Nasser of a huge chunk of his "second circle." But the UAR has not despaired because it has, over the years, sought to champion the cause of Pan-Africanism by various means. One instrument of President Nasser has been Islam. In addition to the 45 million Muslims in the five North African states, there are roughly 45 million south of the Sahara. Five of the African states that are associated with the Common Market are among the African countries with the largest percentages of Muslim population. These are the Republic of Somalia, about 99 per cent Muslim; the Islamic Republic of Mauritania, 98 per cent; Niger, 75 per cent; Senegal, 70 per cent; and Chad, 50 per cent.[20] Islam is utilized by President Nasser in his dealings with African

[17] See Arts. 131–36 of the Treaty of Rome and its Annex IV.

[18] These states are Burundi, the Federal Republic of Cameroon, the Central African Republic, Chad, the Congo Republic (Brazzaville), the Republic of the Congo (Leopoldville), the Ivory Coast, Dahomey, Gabon, Upper Volta, Mali, the Islamic Republic of Mauritania, Niger, Rwanda, Senegal, the Republic of Somalia, and Togo. The Malagasy Republic, formerly the French Overseas Territory of Madagascar, is the eighteenth associated state, lying off the eastern coast of Africa, from which it is separated by the Mozambique Channel.

[19] Information Service, EEC, Washington, D.C., *Convention d'association entre la Communauté économique européenne et les états africains et Malgache associés à cette communauté.*

[20] Jacques Baulin, *The Arab Role in Africa* (Baltimore, 1962), pp. 12–13.

countries, whether or not they are associated with the Common Market and whether or not they have large Muslim populations. It was reported in 1960 that "a resurgence of zeal for conversion to Islam of the colored races has accompanied the winning of political independence and the strong ties of national sentiment. With government according to the principles of Mohammed becoming practical politics, a new vitality is being infused into what is held out to be the Black Man's religion. In this the hand of Cairo exerts strong political pressure." [21]

Another instrument which has been employed in saving what is left of the "second circle" is the campaign against the imperialism and colonialism of the West. With European attempts at unity in mind, the secretary of the Afro-Asian Peoples' Solidarity group stated at a session held in Gaza December 9–11, 1961: "In their desperate attempts against national liberation movements and peace-loving peoples, imperialists are trying to get together and form a united front." In the same session the group passed a resolution regarding the Common Market in Europe directing the Executive Committee to draw "the attention of the Afro-Asian Peoples to the danger of colonialist monopolies that gathered for getting a grip on the markets in Africa and Asia and using Israel as a screen for maintaining their hold on these markets." [22] The subsequent resolution of the Economic Council of the Arab League revealed even more clearly that the United Arab Republic is not only concerned about the African states that are already associated with the Common Market but also wishes to thwart any attempt on the part of the Common Market to win new African associates. The Council decided to keep a close watch on any such attempt.[23]

[21] *New York Times*, March 26, 1960.
[22] See *Afro-Asian Bulletin*, suppl. on the Afro-Asian People's Solidarity Executive Committee, January–February, 1962 (Cairo, 1962), p. 27.
[23] See Khalil, *op. cit.*, pp. 166–67.

"NEOCOLONIALISM"

Arab opposition to the Common Market is also influenced by what is labeled the "neocolonialism" of Western Europe. The Common Market, the Arabs believe, is an economic grouping of a number of European colonial powers which have definite political aims. The Arab objection to the Common Market's political features will be discussed below. Here we shall consider Arab opposition to its economic dangers. Basically their objection revolves about one question. That is the danger inherent in the Common Market to all the underdeveloped countries of the world. Of particular concern is the harm that the Common Market may do to the African associates and all other African states.

The first danger of the Common Market lies in the possibility of its becoming the nucleus of what is called a "General Union" of all the Western European states under the "hegemony of the United States." This could be facilitated by a merger of the Seven and the Six, that is, the Free Trade Area and the Common Market. The economic strength of such a union together with its nuclear capability would enable the "General Union" to establish a "complete monopoly" over the products of the developing countries.[24] Thus the Common Market is suspect on the ground that it seeks to reestablish, in a new guise, the old European colonial domination of the underdeveloped countries.

One aspect of this danger in the Arab view is the status of the African states associated with the Common Market. In fact, what the Arab sees in these countries he takes as substantiating his contention in regard to the global danger of the Common Market. The heart of the Arab's objection to the Common Market is due to what he considers the harmful nature of the relationship between these countries and the Market. This view is shared in some Af-

[24] See Al Ahram al-Iqtisadi, September 15, 1962, p. 12.

rican nationalist circles, and both the Arabs and the African nationalists opposed to the Common Market seem to find comfort in a study by the United Nations Commission for Africa of the effects of the EEC on Africa.[25] Although this study speculates on possible disadvantages of the association, it certainly does not see, as some Arab and African nationalists do, the features of neo-colonialism in the relationship of the African associates and the Common Market.

In the association of the African states with the Common Market the Arabs see a "dangerous plot" by which the metropolitan centers of industry in Europe seek to create and maintain a colonial periphery of producers of raw materials. This would result in a glorified, twentieth-century version of Africans as "hewers of wood and drawers of water." The processes of modernization and industrialization in Africa would be sacrificed to the continuing industrial growth and economic prosperity of the Common Market countries. According to this view, the Common Market projects in the African associated countries which encourage the production of wool, wood, copper, and cocoa are examples of "unhealthy progress" in those countries.[26] This "danger" is also expressed in other terms:

For example, establishing a relationship with the Market, whether on a basis of full membership or association, would mean tying up the economy of the country to the Western economy in matters of national production and foreign trade. This is especially true of African countries because the African economy is underdeveloped and because it depends on exporting agricultural

[25] This study is *The Impact of Western European Integration on African Trade and Development*, Economic and Social Council Document E/CN.14/72. For two other studies of the United Nations, see *Recent Developments in Western European Economic Groupings as Far as They Concern African Countries*, Document E/ON.14/139, and its follow-up Document E/CN.14/139/Add. 2. For a discussion of the problem, see "African Attitudes to the European Economic Community" by Ali A. Mazrui, in *International Affairs*, January, 1963, pp. 24–36.
[26] *Al Ahram al-Iqtisadi*, September 15, 1962, p. 13.

products. This leads to enhancing the state of economic subservience, resulting in specialization in the production of one commodity, which eventually develops into an Exposed Economy. The Common Market is also likely to embark upon economic planning—of a capitalistic nature—in an attempt to mobilize economic, financial, and human resources. The economic plan would have two sides, one spontaneous and genuine in Europe, and the other exploitative in Africa. Economic planning in the Market will amount to putting African resources at the service of Western Europe in accordance with a long-range program. This will paralyze the ability of African states in their dealing with the outside world, East and West. It will also restrict their capacity to protect their growing industry. The Common Market basically will be a club for the wealthy.[27]

The Arab attitude toward the Common Market is influenced not only by the "danger" that is seen in the relationship between the African associates and the Common Market but also in the way that EEC has affected the Afro-Asian countries in general. "With the creation of the Common Market in Europe," states the journal of the Permanent Secretariat of the Afro-Asian Peoples' Solidarity organization, "a big tariff wall has been erected against imports, particularly from Afro-Asian countries. The result is that the exports of cash crops from Afro-Asian countries have fallen and there is a further decline in their prices. Not only that, it has become almost impossible for newly independent countries, which are developing their economy, to export any of their products to the Western Market. In this way the Western Common Market is a big curb on and a hindrance to the development of backward countries. It is an imperialist weapon to hinder the growth and development of the Afro-Asian countries." [28]

The possibility of British accession is also feared on the ground that countries like India, Malaya, Ceylon, Ghana, and Nigeria will be seriously affected. Their exports will fall and their incomes will be further reduced. They already face a serious crisis in their foreign

[27] *Ibid.*, pp. 55–56.　　[28] *Afro-Asian Bulletin*, July–August, 1961, p. 11.

exchange problems. British entry into the Common Market will hamper their growth and development still more. Because of these and other "dangers" that are believed to be inherent in the establishment of the Common Market, it is concluded that the Afro-Asian countries have no alternative but to face this situation and to appreciate to the full that there is only one way to growth and development—namely, to extend and expand mutual trade and mutual help, to emerge from dependence on the West, and to "extend and expand their economic links with countries which are prepared to help them on the basis of equality and mutual benefit." [29]

"POSITIVE NEUTRALISM"

From the foregoing discussion of the factors underlying the Arab attitude toward the Common Market it must be apparent that political rather than economic considerations predominate. This appears most clearly in the way that Arabs discern incompatibilities between their commitment to what is known as "positive neutralism" and the Common Market. No attempt will be made here to analyze the emergence of this phenomenon in Arab foreign policy. It is sufficient to recall that its roots may be easily traced to the early 1950's, when Egypt was seeking the termination of British control in the Suez Canal Zone and when the West was bent upon the creation of some sort of military alliance in the Middle East as exemplified by proposals for the establishment of the Allied Middle East Command and later the Middle East Defense Organization. Egypt, of course, repeatedly rejected all these attempts. [30]

[29] *Ibid.*

[30] For the text of the proposal for an Allied Middle East Command, see the *Department of State Bulletin*, October 22, 1951, pp. 647–48. For the Egyptian rejection of the proposal, see Kamil Abdul Rahim, Egyptian Ambassador to the United States, quoted in Edward Latham (ed.), *Crisis in the Middle East* (New York, 1952), p. 95.

It is important, however, to note that over the years the policy of positive neutralism has acquired a far broader scope than it had at the time of its inception. As a result of exchanges of visits among neutralist leaders such as President Nasser and Prime Minister Nehru and of conferences such as the Bandung Conference, the Afro-Asian Conference, and the Belgrade Conference, to mention the more important ones, the concept of neutralism has grown beyond mere nonalignment with the East or the West. The criteria applied in inviting neutralist states to the Belgrade Conference required that a neutralist country should follow an independent policy based on nonalignment and peaceful coexistence, should support liberation movements, should not be a member of a multilateral military pact or of a bilateral military pact with a Big Power in the context of the East-West struggle, and should not have granted military bases to foreign powers.[31]

Obviously the Common Market is not a military arrangement, but the Arab objection to it is based on the ground that the EEC is a product of the East-West struggle and that it reinforces bipolarism, which is responsible for international tensions, the armament race, and threats to world peace and security. To Arab observers, the ill effects of the Common Market fall most heavily on "positive neutralism" rather than on what is called "classical neutrality," such as that of Switzerland, or on "conventional neutrality," such as that of Austria. The problem is stated by an Egyptian intellectual in these terms:

The more the Common Market expands geographically the weaker the concept of neutrality will become. The Market is an attempt at maintaining bipolarism by wiping out positive neutrality and weakening the African vote in the United Nations. The adverse effects of the Market will be felt particularly on positive neutrality. This is so because countries subscribing

[31] See N. P. Nayar, "A Study of the Policy of Non-alignment, with Special Reference to African Problems," *Foreign Policy Reports*, December, 1961, p. 132.

to classical neutrality can become members in the Market and still retain their negative neutrality.

The neutralist African countries can never retain their positive neutrality, theoretically or actually, because they are underdeveloped and because their products are not diversified. Moreover, they export raw materials to specific countries and import mainly consumer goods. Thus, the adverse effects of the Market on positive neutrality will serve to strengthen the Western Bloc and weaken the Afro-Asian Bloc.[32]

Here, again, it is clearly seen that the attitude of the Arabs toward the Common Market is influenced by their estimation of the impact of EEC on positive neutralism, not merely in the Arab Middle East, but also in Africa. In all the factors analyzed above the opposition of the Arab countries to the Common Market has revealed itself in terms of Arab interests, not only in the Middle East, but also in Africa. The Arab view of the Common Market is basically political and is inextricably linked to the East-West struggle on the one hand and to nationalistic fear and suspicion of Western colonialism and imperialism on the other. The Common Market countries may argue that their relationship with the African associates is motivated not only by self-interest but also by high ideals, but so far this argument has had little or no effect in dissipating Arab fears and suspicion. Perhaps for this reason the Arab countries have so far paid no serious attention to the effects of the Common Market on the exportation of their commodities to the Six. Although Arab literature is replete with all sorts of denunciations of the Common Market, one searches in vain for an objective and thorough assessment of the impact of the Common Market on Arab exports. As this chapter has shown, the Common Market is on the Arab black list if it entertains the notion of eventual Israeli association, but it is also suspect because it seems to rob the Arabs of potential leadership of Pan-Africanism, because it is regarded

[32] See *Al Ahram al-Iqtisadi*, September 25, 1963, pp. 54–55.

as a tool of neocolonialism, and because it is considered incompatible with positive neutralism.

AN ARAB COMMON MARKET

Arab reaction to the European Common Market has not been limited to pressures and threats of countermeasures toward the EEC in the event of Israeli association. The Arab countries have also given renewed attention to the establishment of their own common market. The credit for this goes chiefly to the Lebanese. An Arab common market has been proposed on various grounds. Some believe that the need for strengthening Arab commercial relations has increased to the point where it is now urgent. This need is due to the fact that many Arab states depend heavily on the export of one or two crops the prices of which fluctuate almost constantly, making for unpredictability of income. It is assumed that the establishment of an Arab common market would somehow remedy this situation and thereby increase Arab per capita income. The establishment of such a market together with an Arab development bank "is expected to channel several million dollars from the sale of petroleum into productive means." [33]

An article that appeared recently in a Lebanese paper, *Al-Yawm*, asserted that the idea of an Arab economic community first appeared in 1914; in 1950 the idea was expanded to include the establishment of a free-zone area in the Arab world. The article did admit, however, that except for two agreements on economic cooperation concluded in 1953 the Arab states have not undertaken "any successful effort in the direction of establishing a common market." In trying to convince its readers of the feasibility as well as desirability of establishing an Arab common market, the writer stated:

[33] *Beirut al-Masa*, reprinted in Khalil, *op. cit.*, p. 171.

Arab economies are complementary; most of the Arab states have agricultural economies in which more than two-thirds of their population work. But the agricultural products of these states are varied and are not considered competitive. Lebanon, for example, specializes in fruit, Jordan in vegetables, UAR in cotton, Iraq in dates and grains. . . .

The complementarity of the Arab economies within one market is expected to increase the potentialities for rapid industrial progress. It is generally known that a primary obstacle to industrial growth in the Arab states is their limited local markets. It is all too clear that countries characterized by a small population and a low level of per capita income cannot enjoy the advantages of highly competitive economies. . . . [But] the Arab Common Market will encourage the establishment of a number of medium-size industries which are bound to prosper.[34]

Regardless of the accuracy of the economic analysis of this or other similar sources, the important point is that the Lebanese have generally found it more to their taste to react in this rather positive fashion to the impact of the Common Market in Europe instead of dwelling extensively, as have most of the UAR writers, on the "exploitative plot" of EEC. In this respect one is struck by the fact that, by the admission of a well-known Egyptian writer, it was Lebanon that for many years tried to induce the Arab League to accord major importance to economic cooperation in its work.[35] In fact, Lebanon was also influential in making the Treaty of Joint Defense and Economic Cooperation of 1950 into a treaty, not only of military defense, but of economic cooperation among the Arab states.

Article 7 of this treaty laid the foundation for whatever degree of economic cooperation the Arab states have so far undertaken. On September 9, 1953, two agreements were reached that dealt directly with the problem of Arab economic cooperation. One agreement was concerned with the exchange of goods and services and

[34] *Al-Yawm*, reprinted in *ibid.*, pp. 167–68.
[35] B. Y. Boutros-Ghali, "The Arab League, 1945–1955," *International Conciliation*, May, 1954, p. 434.

the lowering of tariff and trade barriers. It exempted from customs and import duties the agricultural products and livestock of the Arab countries. It also provided for a 25 per cent reduction in customs duties on industrial products; this was later cut to 50 per cent. The other agreement was designed to facilitate both the exchange of currency for the payment of goods and debts and the transfer of capital.

Within the context of these agreements the Arab states have concluded various bilateral trade agreements. Iraq has bilateral agreements with Jordan, Lebanon, Saudi Arabia, and Egypt. Jordan's important trade partners in the Middle East are Lebanon and Syria, and Lebanon's best trading partners in the area are Iraq, Jordan, Saudi Arabia, and Syria. Within the framework of the two general agreements Egypt has signed bilateral agreements with Iraq, Lebanon, and Saudi Arabia. Jordan is the leading intra-Arab trader of the Middle East, followed by Lebanon and Syria. Egypt's share of the intra-Arab trade is small.[36]

Intra-Arab trade is, in general, small because Arab economies are competitive in spite of the belief of some Arab economists to the contrary.[37] A study by the Working Party for the Middle East under the auspices of the Food and Agriculture Organization of the United Nations stated:

While the elements of diversity are not completely lacking, the greater part of the region is in the arid zone and produces the same range of field crops, notably wheat, barley and cotton, and fruit and vegetables, and also the same kinds of livestock. A second factor impeding the expansion of trade within the region is that the economies of the Near East countries are primarily agricultural, and are not complementary to any considerable degree. However, this factor may gradually become less important as a result of the growing diversity in the stage of development reached following the im-

[36] For details, see UN, *Economic Developments in the Middle East, 1959–1961* (New York, 1962), pp. 90–96.
[37] Khalil, *op. cit.*, pp. 167–68.

plementation of development programs and measures now in effect in various parts of the region. It would, however, be desirable that governments continue to give much attention to a closer co-ordination of their development programs. A striking trend in the agricultural policies of Near Eastern countries in recent years is the growing tendency toward self-sufficiency in basic foodstuffs and other agricultural products. Such a trend is not easily reconciled with efforts toward a freer movement of supplies within the region.[38]

Since 1956 when this report was written, there has been no significant change in the major obstacles to intra-Arab trade. Being in an arid zone, the region still produces the same range of field crops. In fact, the most recent United Nations analysis of Middle East agricultural problems reveals that production has been adversely affected in spite of the fact that in recent years many countries have made special efforts to increase agricultural production and raise productivity through various development schemes, the use of tractors, and the application of fertilizers.[39] The second obstacle to intraregional trade—the fact that the Arab economies are not complementary—also remains the same as before. In fact, this is reflected in the gradually deteriorating trade. In viewing these problems together with the heavy dependence of the Middle East's predominantly agrarian economies on the "vagaries of weather," the United Nations survey observes:

While the region as a whole seems to have fared relatively well in the face of prolonged drought conditions, individual countries have had to cope with serious losses in their staple products and even in their cash crops. When this unpleasant fact is viewed in the context of a rapidly growing population and gradually deteriorating terms of trade, the magnitude of the problem of feeding the population of the area and meeting the investment requirements of development programmes becomes obvious.[40]

[38] Food and Agriculture Organization, UN, *Selected Problems of Production and Trade in the Near East* (Rome, 1956), p. 9.
[39] UN, *Economic Developments M.E.*, 1959–1961, pp. 11–12.
[40] *Ibid.*, p. 14.

"The striking trend" toward self-sufficiency in food crops that was reported by the Working Party in 1956 has not only continued in recent years, but has actually been augmented. Even a cursory glance at the recently formulated five-year plans of Iraq, Syria, Jordan, Lebanon, and Egypt reveals with abundant clarity that in the main these plans have been aimed at self-sufficiency in foodstuffs in individual Arab countries rather than at a freer movement of supplies within the region.[41] Whether the European Common Market will prompt the Arab countries to see the inconsistency between their ideal of an Arab common market and their current agricultural policies or will reinforce the continuing trend toward self-sufficiency remains to be seen.

[41] For a summary of these plans, see *ibid.*, pp. 16–23.

VIII

Implications and Reactions

IN THE foregoing pages an attempt has been made to analyze, in broad terms, the impact of the Common Market on Middle East exports by identifying the area's major items of export to the Common Market and by discussing the effects of the EEC policies on such exports. The factors underlying the attitude of the Middle East countries toward the Common Market have been discussed, and the policies actually pursued have been pointed out. The descriptive generalizations that follow are based upon the analyses embodied in the preceding chapters.

IMPLICATIONS

The impact of the Common Market on Middle East exports of oil and petroleum products has been examined in terms of the EEC's emerging energy policy as guided by its energy requirements and the set of principles adopted by the European Parliament and endorsed by the Executives of the ECSC, Euratom, and the Common Market. This impact can make itself felt through the Community's determination to substitute other sources of energy for oil as far as possible, to diversify its sources of energy, to adopt a common tariff for petroleum products, and to obtain inexpensive supplies of oil. The problem of substitution may be reduced to the utilization of nuclear energy, which will pose no serious competition to oil exports of the Middle East before 1975, and even after that date the Common Market's dependence on oil as a source of energy will continue. Nor does the tariff system of the Common Market present any problem for Middle East crude oil exports. Petroleum products of the area will be subjected to the common external tariff although indications are that this tariff will be quite low.

Diversification of sources of supply poses a rather serious problem, particularly if France succeeds in obtaining special preference for Algerian oil in the Common Market. Perhaps the most serious disagreement between the Middle East oil-exporting countries and the Common Market will arise as the result of the EEC's determination to secure cheap oil supplies. Inasmuch as the economic development projects of these countries are heavily dependent on revenues from oil, they are bound to oppose the EEC's oil policy in this respect. The opposition will probably be expressed by individual oil-exporting countries, by the Organization of Petroleum Exporting Countries and the Arab Petroleum Congress, or by a combination of these.

The Middle East grains that are affected are principally barley, wheat, and rice. The impact is felt mainly through the establishment of the new levy system, through the acceleration of intra-Community trade in these commodities, and through the EEC's association with the African states. Germany is the chief importer of barley and wheat, and its levies on these commodities during the rest of the transition period will probably prove higher than they were in the pre-Market days. The duties imposed by the Common Market levy system will, in the last analysis, depend upon the level of prices within the Community, before and after the full emergence of the single external levy in 1970.

Vegetables and fruits constitute a most important part of Middle East nonpetroleum exports to the Common Market. The effects of the Common Market will be felt not merely through the progressive introduction of the common external tariff, but also through the new and rigorous quality standards which may adversely affect the volume of exports unless the Middle East exporters of these commodities abandon their careless packing practices. More important, Middle East exporters may suddenly find their exports suspended or subjected to a "countervailing charge" if their prices fall below "a reference price." The most important challenge to Middle East exporters of vegetables and fruits will stem from two additional sources. One is the rapid growth of trade in these commodities within the Community, as exemplified by the greater availability of Italian citrus fruits on the Community's markets at the expense of Israeli citrus fruit exports. The other is through the preferential treatment accorded exports to the Common Market from Greece, an associated state. This is particularly serious for Iran and Turkey, which are the leading exporters of dried fruits to the EEC. However, there are encouraging indications that the interests of these two countries will be protected —those of Iran by a commercial agreement with the EEC and those of Turkey by association.

Middle East exports of cotton, tobacco, and carpets to the EEC could be significantly affected. The common external tariff on cotton will be nil, but a challenge to Middle East exports of cotton to the Common Market may be posed by the greater availability of cotton from Greece and particularly from the African associates of the EEC. Unless the association agreement is ratified, the exports of Turkish tobacco will suffer in two ways. The common external tariff on tobacco will be high by 1970, and the gradual approach to that tariff during the transition period can prove disadvantageous to Turkey. Turkish tobacco exports to the Common Market may also suffer as the result of the preferential treatment that Italian and Greek tobacco may enjoy in the Common Market. Iranian rug exports face serious challenge, principally as the result of the high common external tariff. There is every reason to believe, however, that Iranian interests will be protected by the commercial agreement just signed between Tehran and Brussels.

Britain's entry into the Common Market, in the absence of some kind of agreement between the individual Middle Eastern countries and the Common Market, would aggravate the export problem of a number of commodities. The most important of these would be Israeli citrus fruits. British accession to the Treaty of Rome in the absence of an Israeli agreement with the Common Market would seriously damage the economy of Israel. Turkey could also suffer seriously, if it does not succeed in becoming an associate member, particularly so far as its exports of tobacco to Britain are concerned. If the common external tariffs on petroleum products are set high, which is doubtful, Iran and Kuwait, the leading exporters of such products to the United Kingdom, would be adversely affected.

POLICIES AND ATTITUDES

The economic effects of the Common Market have played a dominant role in shaping the attitudes of the non-Arab countries of Iran, Israel, and Turkey toward the Common Market. Other considerations, more political and psychological in nature, have also influenced the policies of these countries toward the EEC. Iran's policy derives to no small extent from its geographic proximity to Russia and its bitter memories of past commercial experiences with its northern neighbor. Iran wishes to avoid any trade difficulty with the West that might force it to trade too extensively with the Soviet Union. Furthermore, Iran is today officially subscribing to the policy of "positive nationalism," which is basically one of alliance with the West as symbolized by Iran's adherence to CENTO and its bilateral defense agreement with the United States. These considerations have inclined Iran toward a policy of accommodation with the Common Market which has resulted in the initialing of a temporary commercial agreement to take effect in January, 1964.

Economic considerations have been most important in Turkey's policy toward the Common Market because Turkey is the leading Middle East exporter of nonpetroleum products to that market. But other considerations are also influential in Turkey's conciliatory policy. Turkey considers itself a European country and has persistently sought membership in European organizations. Furthermore, Turkey without any qualms has cast its lot with the West and is simultaneously a member of NATO and CENTO, linking the defense lines of the West in Asia with Europe. For these reasons Turkey has sought association with the Common Market, and there is every reason to believe that this objective will be achieved. Once this goal is attained, Turkey will be the first and only Middle East country associated with the EEC.

Whether Turkey and Iran, under the impact of the European Common Market, will form their own common market with Pakistan, within the framework of CENTO or otherwise, will remain to be seen. One basic difficulty in the way of such a market is the predominantly agricultural and noncomplementary economies of these countries. This problem could probably be mitigated somewhat if the development programs of these countries were closely coordinated. It is encouraging to note that a greater degree of emphasis is now placed on trade and economic development in CENTO. Attempts at unification and simplification of customs formalities and facilitation of travel and residence by tourists and businessmen through the abolition of visa fees could signal a healthy beginning, particularly when these measures are combined with expansion of regional transportation and telecommunication systems.

The unremitting efforts of Israel to reach a mutually satisfactory agreement with the Common Market are to no small extent the result of the vital significance of West European markets for its products. But Israel is motivated by other considerations also. In the face of the Arab economic boycott it could prove disastrous if Israeli exports were barred from the markets of the Six and the United Kingdom. Conversely, if Israel should have unimpeded access to the rapidly growing markets of Western Europe, it will possibly be able to overcome many of its current economic difficulties. Israel will probably aim at future association with the Common Market, although at the present time it is satisfied with an agreement falling short of association. Current economic differences between the EEC and Israel should not be allowed to overshadow the more important historical and cultural ties of Israel with the West and Israel's silent commitment to the defense of the free world.

Although the economic implications of the Common Market for the Arab countries are by no means without significance, political, ideological, and psychological considerations have played the most important role in shaping Arab attitudes toward the EEC. The most important factor influencing the attitude of the Arabs so far has been the desire to prevent any development that might possibly weaken the effect of their boycott against Israel. Israel is regarded as the arch enemy of the Arabs, and Common Market acceptance of Israeli association will be considered not only an unfriendly act but an act of aggression. Association of Israel with the Common Market, the Arabs believe, will weaken the boycott and strengthen the economy of Israel, with the result that Israeli attraction for Africans will become even greater.

The United Arab Republic in particular is not only opposed to the activities of Israel in Africa but is also resentful of the association of the African countries with the Common Market, in part because this tends to deprive President Nasser of his role as champion of the cause of African nationalism and unity in the associated countries. The appeal to Islam as an instrument of Egyptian policy and charges of Western colonialism and imperialism may still prove ineffective if the African associates find their economic ties with the Common Market far more attractive than the promises emanating from Cairo.

The Arab opposition to the Common Market, again particularly Egyptian opposition, stems also from other considerations. The Common Market is regarded as an instrument of neocolonialism. It is thought to be a grouping of nations that is not only harmful to the African associates but also to the entire underdeveloped world. It is a "dangerous plot" by which the industrial center of Europe seeks to make colonial dependencies out of the developing countries, which will be doomed forever to the status of "hewers of wood and drawers of water." It is a device by which the industrially rich countries of Western Europe seek to continue their former colonial exploitation in a new guise. It is a selfish and exclusive "club of the wealthy countries" that wishes to keep the poor nations down through a monopoly of their resources and the creation of obstacles in the way of their industrialization and modernization.

The Common Market is also suspect because it is believed to be basically incompatible with "positive neutralism." Doctrinaire neutralism repudiates military alignments, and its proponents believe that an institution such as the Common Market renders it impossible for those associated with it to pursue a truly independent policy in the Cold War. They fear that through the back door of commercial ties and economic aid any country associating with the Common Market will inevitably become aligned with the West and thereby lose its freedom of action in return for the illusory material benefits that such an association offers.

Arab suspicion of the West has narrowed the range of alternatives. In their confrontation with the Common Market, many

Arabs suggest two possible courses of action. One is the establishment of an Arab common market. This course is favored by the moderates, among whom many Lebanese can be found. The overall appeal of the idea of an Arab common market stems from the long-cherished desire for Arab unity. Many Arabs believe that such a move is not only politically desirable but would also be economically beneficial. They seem, however, to underestimate the difficulty inherent in the nature of the economies of the Arab countries which are more competitive than complementary. Should the Arab countries closely coordinate their economic development programs, this difficulty could be overcome to some extent. At present, an obsession with self-sufficiency rather than a dedication to common interests marks every Arab development program of any significance.

The other course of action often suggested is to extend and expand economic links with those countries which are prepared to help the Arabs "on the basis of equality and mutual benefit." It is obvious from the context of these suggestions that the allusion is to the countries of the Eastern bloc. When the advocates of such a view are asked whether the extension of such ties with the countries of the Soviet bloc or Comecon (Council of Mutual Economic Assistance, the economic alliance of the Soviet bloc) might not invite the same kind of political problems that are feared from association with the Common Market, the answer is invariably in the negative, not so much because they trust the Soviet Union but because they distrust the West.

THE BROADER QUESTIONS

This basic distrust raises two related questions. One pertains to the immediate problem of the Cold War and the impact of the Common Market on the Arab Middle East. Arab suspicion of the West obviously predates the establishment of the EEC and is rooted in Arab disillusionment with Britain and France and subsequently with the United States. The fact is that the establishment of the Common Market has given rise to fresh suspicions, which must be counteracted. The Common Market consists of only six countries of the West, but the image that it produces in the strategic Middle East will ultimately affect us all. This is why the nature of its policies must be of concern to both sides of the Atlantic. If the Common Market preaches free trade and practices protectionism, if it preaches interdependence and practices provincialism, it may well become an additional instrument of alienation of the Arab Middle East. The Soviet bloc takes comfort in the Arab charges that the Common Market is an instrument of neo-colonialism, a weapon of imperialism, and a "plot of the monopolists," and we must show the absurdity of these charges by action. Before we can do this we must first put our house in order by reemphasizing the Atlantic spirit that, through the Marshall Plan, set in motion the forces that have produced the Common Market.

The second question pertains to the creation of a spirit of trust and cooperation between the West and the Middle East *as a whole* regardless of the exigencies of the Cold War. So far the EEC experiment has tended to aggravate and catalyze indigenous tension and ferment, to exacerbate divisions between Arab and non-Arab states, to further polarize attitudes of the Middle East countries not only toward the EEC but also toward the Atlantic Community, and to provide fresh impetus to Arab-Israeli conflict in the Middle East and to Arab-Israeli rivalry in Africa. The reduction of these divisions and tensions within the Middle East and between the Arab Middle East and the West is a worthy objective. It is an objective that looks to the distant future, to that future which should witness the rise of an Atlantic–Middle East community.

Such a community could, hopefully, become the nucleus of a new world legal and political order. Apart from geographic proximity, the Middle East and Western Europe are interdependent with regard to petroleum, and the Middle East belongs with the West historically and culturally. The Declaration of Paris issued by the delegates to the Atlantic Convention of NATO Nations recalled this historic-cultural reality in its preamble by stating that "the Atlantic peoples are heir to a magnificent civilization whose origins include the early achievements of the Near East." The European Economic Community can become a most effective instrument for dispelling the current suspicions of the Arabs. It can demonstrate that the European Economic Community will not jeopardize Arab economic interests and standards of living, but that, conversely, it will provide the Arab as well as other underdeveloped countries of the world with unprecedented trade opportunities as well as capital and technical know-how.

It is encouraging to note that the United States has insisted, in its negotiations with the EEC, that any tariff reductions that the United States may obtain from the Common Market should be extended to all other qualified nations in the world who wish to adjust their trade policies accordingly. In his address of June 25, 1963, at the Paulskirche in Frankfurt, Germany, President Kennedy stressed the world-wide responsibility of the Atlantic Community:

Indeed, economic cooperation is needed throughout the entire free world. By opening our markets to the developing countries of Africa, Asia and Latin America, by contributing our capital and skills, by stabilizing basic prices, we can help assure them of a favorable climate for freedom and growth. This is an Atlantic responsibility. For the Atlantic nations themselves helped to awaken these peoples. Our merchants and our traders ploughed up their soils—and their societies as well—in search of minerals and oil and rubber and coffee. Now we must help them gain full membership in the 20th century, closing the gap between the rich and the poor.

Only a few months after the Common Market began effective operation the United States publicly declared its willingness to assist the Arab countries in their multilateral efforts toward economic development. On August 13, 1958, President Eisenhower proposed to the General Assembly of the United Nations that consultations with the Arab nations of the Middle East be undertaken immediately by the Secretary-General for the establishment of an Arab development institution *governed by the Arab states* and supported by their own resources. The United States would be prepared to aid this institution, whose function would be to provide loans as well as the technical assistance required in the formulation of development projects. The West is in a far better position today to give meaning to this proposal because in the intervening years the Common Market has become an economic giant on the other side of the Atlantic. Once the United States and the Common Market begin, as they must, to act as partners rather than rivals, they can share the burden of assisting the Arabs to stand on their own feet.

In doing this we must convince the Arab countries by our actions that they would not have to become the tail of our political or military kite in order to receive our assistance in gaining their goal of an Arab common market and eventual Arab unity. We must demonstrate that European unity and Atlantic Community are not incompatible with their aspirations of creating a United Arab States for the betterment of their people socially and economically. We must assist the Arab countries in the gigantic task of regaining self-respect, in rebuilding their culture, in redefining their universe, and in finding their identity in it.

No amount of goodwill on the part of the EEC or even the Atlantic Community as a whole will be sufficient by itself to usher in a new era of cooperation between the Middle East and the West. The Arab Middle East bears equal, if not greater, responsibility for the creation of that atmosphere of trust which is so essential for any kind of cooperation between the two areas. The Arab Middle East will have to develop a more reasoned perspective not only as to the character of the EEC experiment but also as to the motives and actions of the West in general. It will have to promote internal conditions favorable for more fruitful cooperation in economic development. It will also have to demonstrate that its own aspirations for an Arab Community are not incompatible with the values of the Atlantic Community.

APPENDIX TABLES

Note on the Tables

THE tables included in the Appendix serve two primary purposes: (1) to document the description and analysis embodied in the text and (2) to provide the interested reader with more detailed statistical data than those given in the text. The data on exports of the countries of the Middle East to the Common Market countries and the United Kingdom are compiled from the data on imports reported by these countries because such data are more complete and uniform than those from the various Middle Eastern countries.

The value of the oil exports of the four leading Middle East oil-exporting countries (Tables 4–7) to the Common Market is given in terms of crude oil and petroleum products because the EEC makes such a distinction for tariff purposes. To show the trend in oil exports to the EEC, the three years prior to the establishment of the Common Market are included. The fourth year is a post-Market year and the latest for which data are available.

The over-all value of the exports to the Common Market of the seven major Middle Eastern exporters is given in seven tables (Tables 8–14), one for each country covering a seven-year period, to indicate the general trend before and after the establishment of

119

the Common Market. For the oil-exporting countries these tables include the value of their nonpetroleum products as well as that of their crude oil and petroleum products.

Tables 15–21 provide data on the quantity and value of the non-petroleum exports of the Middle East to the Common Market countries in three specific years prior to the establishment of the Common Market. The selection of these export items has been guided by two considerations: (1) inclusion of those commodities that have consistently been of particular significance in the exports of the Middle East to the Common Market countries and (2) in-clusion of those export items for which the Common Market has already formulated policies or has adopted principles to govern fu-ture policies. Obviously, the purpose of these tables is not to pro-vide exhaustive accounts of the exports of the Middle East coun-tries to the Common Market. The reader is referred to the valuable analytical tables prepared by the Statistical Office of the European Communities which are cited in the footnotes of several of the tables included in this work. Table 22 gives the 1961 value of the export items treated in Tables 15–21. This table is included in or-der to provide a basis for comparison (1) with the pre-Market years in respect to the nonpetroleum exports and (2) with the years subsequent to the inauguration of the Agricultural Policy (January, 1962) in respect to agricultural exports.

Table 23 is provided in order to indicate, in broad terms, the value of the major nonpetroleum exports of the Middle East to the United Kingdom. The commodities are the same as those exported to the Common Market countries. The value of oil exports is given in Tables 4–7. No data for post-Market years have been provided because Great Britain is not yet a member of the EEC.

TABLE 1

Proven oil reserves in the Middle East, by country
(millions of barrels)

Country	Proven reserves	Percentage of world total
Bahrain	245	0.1
Iran	35,000	11.3
Iraq	26,500	8.6
Israel	34	—
Kuwait	62,000	20.0
Neutral Zone	6,000	1.9
Qatar	2,750	0.9
Saudi Arabia	52,000	16.8
Syria	100	—
Trucial Coast	3,500	1.1
Turkey	75	—
UAR (Egypt)	710	0.2
Middle East total	188,914	60.9
World total	309,975	100.0

Source: Data from *Oil and Gas Journal* (Tulsa, Okla.), January 29, 1962.

121

TABLE 2

World production of crude petroleum, by region
(thousands of tons and percentages)

Region	1958	1959	1960	1961 [a]	% of world total, 1961	% of change, 1961 over 1958
Middle East	215,002	231,574	265,112	282,296	25.2	31.3
North America	353,320	372,900	373,963	384,200	34.3	8.7
Latin America	176,227	188,662	197,672	202,055	18.1	14.7
Eastern Europe [b]	126,750	143,592	162,653	181,650	16.2	43.3
Far East [c]	25,502	29,319	32,293	33,425	3.0	31.1
Western Europe	12,112	12,931	14,108	15,065	1.3	24.4
Africa	1,358	2,809	10,668	19,720	1.8	1,352.1
World total	910,300	981,800	1,056,800	1,118,900	100.0	22.9

Source: UN, *Economic Developments in the Middle East, 1959–1961: Supplement to World Economic Survey, 1961* (New York, 1962), p. 135.

[a] Estimates.
[b] Including the Soviet Union and Yugoslavia.
[c] Including Mainland China.

122

TABLE 3

Destination of Middle Eastern crude petroleum exports
(thousands of tons)

Region & year	Total Middle East	Iran	Iraq	Kuwait [a]	Saudi Arabia
WORLD					
1958	176,400	24,200	33,800	67,300	41,740
1959	189,100	28,750	39,300	66,560	45,480
1960	216,200	33,420	45,200	77,840	50,750
1961	237,080	41,550	46,590	81,240	56,850
Other Middle East					
1958	13,750	2,500	2,280	1,220	7,390
1959	13,930	1,460	1,830	2,640	7,940
1960	16,340	1,820	1,220	3,220	9,930
1961	18,280	2,930	1,910	2,060	10,550
Western Europe					
1958	109,500	14,600	26,500	42,150	19,600
1959	119,720	18,620	31,810	40,180	22,610
1960	134,200	20,900	37,280	48,020	23,240
1961	141,160	24,020	38,260	49,750	22,790
Bel-Lux					
1958	6,220	2,740	600	1,470	1,400
1959	6,200	2,320	1,700	910	1,270
1960	6,410	1,920	2,230	740	1,520
1961	6,230	2,420	2,750	210	760
France					
1958	24,950	1,500	8,300	8,500	3,740
1959	24,700	2,010	9,240	7,200	3,100
1960	21,300	1,400	7,820	7,450	2,980
1961	20,340	810	6,890	8,710	2,330
Germany					
1958	8,840	910	3,070	1,900	2,970
1959	13,840	3,000	3,870	1,740	5,230
1960	18,610	5,420	4,540	1,520	6,060
1961	21,840	10,000	4,160	2,200	3,710
Italy					
1958	20,680	520	4,830	6,900	5,900
1959	21,960	1,500	5,320	7,470	6,180
1960	24,690	1,430	7,980	8,490	5,820
1961	26,990	1,300	8,950	9,040	6,230

[a] Including exports of the Neutral Zone.

123

TABLE 3 (continued)

Region & year	Total Middle East	Iran	Iraq	Kuwait [a]	Saudi Arabia
Netherlands					
1958	11,400	1,580	1,800	5,800	1,720
1959	10,160	500	1,820	5,350	2,190
1960	13,640	1,180	3,260	6,400	2,600
1961	14,460	1,200	5,440	4,850	2,900
Far East					
1958	18,850	2,150	3,770	5,710	6,980
1959	22,640	3,060	4,460	7,710	7,300
1960	29,720	4,040	5,280	12,670	7,120
1961	36,190	5,710	4,200	16,050	9,550
North America					
1958	21,700	900	1,230	13,900	5,440
1959	21,340	2,080	1,200	12,600	5,420
1960	22,970	3,810	1,090	10,770	6,330
1961	23,180	4,500	1,180	10,350	5,840
Oceania [b]					
1958	6,350	2,600		1,000	740
1959	6,420	2,290		1,070	690
1960	7,500	1,550	330	1,530	1,630
1961	8,220	2,870	770	1,620	1,420
Other America					
1958	4,090			3,280	810
1959	3,390			2,360	1,030
1960	2,810			1,620	1,180
1961	4,190		50	1,400	2,740
Africa [c]					
1958	1,300	1,300			
1959	1,290	1,230			60
1960	1,300	1,300			
1961	1,940	1,480	200		260

Source: UN, *World Energy Supplies, 1958–1961* (New York, 1963), pp. 90–95.

[a] Including exports of the Neutral Zone.
[b] Imports of Australia.
[c] Mainly imports of South Africa.

TABLE 4

Iran's oil exports to the EEC and the United Kingdom
(in thousands of dollars)

	1952		1954		1956		1961	
	Petroleum crude	Petroleum products	Petroleum crude	Petroleum products	Petroleum crude	Petroleum products	Petroleum crude	Petroleum products
Bel-Lux	$1,228	$ 122	$ 314		$23,245	$ 76	$ 47,552	$ 228
France		294	751		40,627		15,042	1,879
Germany					3,002	212	187,875	378
Italy		2,993	7,105	$1,084	8,560	547	21,808	559
Netherlands					18,006	365	25,347	1,139
EEC total	$1,228	$3,409	$8,170	$1,084	$93,440	$1,200	$297,624	$4,183
United Kingdom			$ 339		$74,829	$7,839	$108,174	$5,470

Source: UN, *Commodity Trade Statistics*, 1952, 1954, 1956, and 1961 (New York, 1953, 1955, 1957, and 1962).

TABLE 5

Iraq's oil exports to the EEC and the United Kingdom
(in thousands of dollars)

	1952 Petroleum crude	1952 Petroleum products	1954 Petroleum crude	1954 Petroleum products	1956 Petroleum crude	1956 Petroleum products	1961 Petroleum crude	1961 Petroleum products
Bel-Lux	$ 16,609		$ 17,298		$ 27,306		$ 47,762	$5,558
France	149,073		221,195		206,914	$1,658	129,238	
Germany	34,544		35,798		54,386	31	79,203	
Italy	54,694		119,629	$159	157,177	242	153,475	1,619
Netherlands	11,662		1,183		4,181		2,664	
EEC total	$266,582		$395,103	$159	$449,964	$1,931	$412,342	$7,177
United Kingdom	$115,660		$118,591		$ 62,980		$122,053	

Source: Same as Table 4.

TABLE 6

Saudi Arabian oil exports to the EEC and the United Kingdom
(in thousands of dollars)

	1952		1954		1956		1961	
	Petroleum crude	Petroleum products	Petroleum crude	Petroleum products	Petroleum crude	Petroleum products	Petroleum crude	Petroleum products
Bel-Lux	$128,558			$1,041	$ 17,964	$1,772	$ 11,101	
France	33,298	$ 676	$ 75,302	974	60,774	3,303	45,271	$1,623
Germany	92,201	1,311	56,109		70,139	3,606	72,240	
Italy		2,411	94,887	131	105,137	325	100,886	646
Netherlands	441		370		5,955	992	31,820	174
EEC total	$254,498	$4,398	$226,668	$2,146	$259,969	$9,998	$261,318	$2,443
United Kingdom	$ 98,749		$ 3,546	$1,112	$ 13,823		$ 35,874	$ 135

Source: Same as Table 4.

127

TABLE 7

Other Arabian oil exports to the EEC and the United Kingdom[a]

(in thousands of dollars)

	1952 Petroleum crude	1952 Petroleum products	1954 Petroleum crude	1954 Petroleum products	1956 Petroleum crude	1956 Petroleum products	1961 Petroleum crude	1961 Petroleum products
Bel-Lux	$ 42,406	$ 256	$ 38,001		$ 26,169	$ 2,761	$ 3,621	$ 192
France	242,462		175,236		210,665	646	159,263	1,577
Germany	13,146		22,426		70,139	1,021	35,409	
Italy	50,787	219	59,877	$ 463	85,316	1,299	136,501	2,911
Netherlands	115,091	33	104,573	16	90,889	2,296	102,176	1,722
EEC total	$463,892	$ 508	$400,113	$ 479	$483,178	$ 8,023	$436,970	$6,402
United Kingdom	$408,421	$6,925	$411,822	$10,886	$381,116	$38,333	$452,179	$7,258

Source: Same as Table 4.

[a] These figures exclude Iran and Iraq, but they include Kuwait (which was separately specified in the source for the first time in 1961) and in some instances probably also Saudi Arabia.

TABLE 8

Egypt's exports to the Common Market
(in thousands of dollars)

Destination	1953	1954	1955	1956	1957	1958	1961
Bel-Lux	$ 6,327	$ 6,249	$ 5,691	$ 4,535	$ 7,346	$ 4,770	$ 5,799
France	51,769	46,346	38,557	34,029	23,972	13,300	13,536
Germany	25,331	33,581	31,967	25,841	26,380	20,221	24,494
Italy	33,062	28,116	20,766	24,947	16,002	26,722	33,565
Netherlands	7,716	6,887	7,729	6,376	4,685	4,603	5,915
EEC total	$124,205	$121,179	$104,710	$95,728	$78,385	$69,616	$83,309

Source: Statistical Office of the European Communities, *Yearbook 1953–1958 of Foreign Trade by Country of Origin and Destination* (Brussels, 1959) and *Foreign Trade Statistics: Analytical Tables—Imports, January–December 1961* (Brussels, 1962).

TABLE 9

Iran's exports (including petroleum) to the Common Market
(in thousands of dollars)

Destination	1953	1954	1955	1956	1957	1958	1961
Bel-Lux	$ 1,571	$ 1,429	$ 9,380	$ 24,630	$ 50,099	$ 69,623	$ 51,158
France	3,669	9,046	36,290	54,837	64,686	46,433	28,656
Germany	24,487	19,023	26,430	28,108	39,081	60,991	226,803
Italy	5,026	12,928	15,088	18,952	20,934	15,302	28,772
Netherlands	2,216	1,927	17,573	20,231	29,257	48,277	29,279
EEC total	$36,969	$44,353	$104,761	$146,758	$204,057	$240,626	$364,668

Source: Same as Table 8.

129

TABLE 10

Iraq's exports (including petroleum) to the Common Market
(in thousands of dollars)

Destination	1953	1954	1955	1956	1957	1958	1961
Bel-Lux	$ 22,860	$ 19,901	$ 32,575	$ 29,187	$ 5,246	$ 8,555	$ 47,878
France	192,637	221,580	226,446	209,463	115,270	180,100	134,953
Germany	36,248	43,096	57,053	61,601	40,287	75,654	79,752
Italy	115,088	130,856	150,223	162,880	81,415	99,991	155,791
Netherlands	13,738	8,956	6,114	6,063	3,554	15,808	3,016
ECC total	$380,571	$424,389	$472,411	$469,194	$245,772	$380,108	$421,390

Source: Same as Table 8.

TABLE 11

Israel's exports to the Common Market
(in thousands of dollars)

Destination	1953	1954	1955	1956	1957	1958	1961
Bel-Lux	$1,347	$2,890	$ 3,976	$ 5,342	$ 7,917	$ 4,343	$15,224
France	337	1,991	2,183	4,383	5,019	5,660	3,927
Germany	106	1,807	1,974	5,674	8,311	11,067	28,842
Italy	321	212	841	1,404	2,551	3,467	12,076
Netherlands	1,631	2,860	3,118	2,633	4,199	4,853	5,575
EEC total	$3,742	$9,760	$12,092	$19,436	$27,997	$29,390	$65,644

Source: Same as Table 8.

TABLE 12

Lebanon's exports to the Common Market
(in thousands of dollars)

Destination	1953	1954	1955	1956	1957	1958	1961
Bel-Lux	$10,225	$24,711	$24,510	$19,554	$ 11,166	$17,348	$ 5,975
France	6,746	3,063	3,223	8,700	11,948	6,248	1,003
Germany	847	823	1,859	2,890	4,045	3,450	1,591
Italy	3,864	1,234	3,887	3,450	6,545	1,419	3,024
Netherlands	47,323	58,197	43,733	34,773	69,041	32,177	45,622
EEC total	$69,005	$88,028	$77,212	$69,367	$102,745	$60,642	$57,215

Source: Same as Table 8.

TABLE 13

Syria's exports to the Common Market
(in thousands of dollars)

Destination	1953	1954	1955	1956	1957	1958	1961
Bel-Lux	$ 5,677	$ 5,951	$ 3,383	$ 5,039	$ 4,467	$ 1,838	$ 7,148
France	18,294	21,523	31,869	23,629	15,663	18,452	8,891
Germany	9,826	20,993	9,342	12,162	8,280	8,338	4,954
Italy	9,160	4,392	11,041	8,243	17,443	15,123	5,248
Netherlands	4,214	15,005	7,392	6,648	7,039	20,916	101,654
EEC total	$47,171	$67,864	$63,027	$55,721	$52,892	$64,667	$127,895

Source: Same as Table 8.

132

TABLE 14

Turkey's exports to the Common Market
(*in thousands of dollars*)

Destination	1953	1954	1955	1956	1957	1958	1961
Bel-Lux	$ 4,090	$ 3,545	$ 6,599	$ 3,907	$ 4,839	$ 4,150	$ 12,305
France	20,120	14,503	24,534	16,526	25,947	18,288	18,147
Germany	77,873	71,650	67,234	67,125	48,897	53,159	77,378
Italy	56,752	23,821	29,272	34,282	32,296	14,392	39,170
Netherlands	5,521	6,597	8,379	7,564	6,226	4,246	5,881
ECC total	$164,356	$120,116	$136,018	$129,404	$118,205	$94,235	$152,881

Source: Same as Table 8.

TABLE 15

Major Egyptian exports to the Common Market
(V in thousands of dollars; Q in metric tons)

Destination	1952 Q	1952 V	1954 Q	1954 V	1956 Q	1956 V
COTTON RAW						
Bel-Lux	2,076	$ 2,341	4,502	$ 4,712	2,816	$ 2,793
France	37,739	50,505	39,514	44,588	27,905	30,908
Germany	22,550	27,056	26,212	28,923	15,247	16,509
Italy	30,836	43,887	23,518	26,875	19,498	23,396
Netherlands	2,404	3,119	4,195	4,314	3,599	3,997
RICE						
Bel-Lux			123	$ 17	129	$ 18
France						
Germany			1,775	260	18,796	2,127
Italy						
Netherlands			99	16		
VEGETABLES FRESH DRY						
Bel-Lux	2,007	$ 199	5,855	$ 347	7,212	$ 536
France	5,105	501	8,137	358	15,892	1,353
Germany	9,921	1,022	35,611	1,970	47,153	3,673
Italy			730	87	3,206	283
Netherlands	1,612	158	3,958	196	11,373	879

Source: UN, *Commodity Trade Statistics*, 1952, 1954, and 1956 (New York, 1953, 1955, and 1957).

TABLE 16

Major Iranian exports (excluding petroleum) to the Common Market

(V in thousands of dollars; Q in metric tons)

Destination	1952 Q	1952 V	1954 Q	1954 V	1956 Q	1956 V
FRUIT NUTS FRESH						
Bel-Lux	124	$ 32				
France					160	$ 312
Germany	437	357	1,139	$ 574	1,982	2,090
Italy						
Netherlands	282	107	104	19	49	38
DRIED FRUIT						
Bel-Lux	64	$ 22	43	$ 15	107	$ 40
France	1,980	707	1,561	501	2,871	1,238
Germany	12,450	3,326	18,817	4,252	20,983	5,923
Italy	100	21			62	16
Netherlands	1,472	415	3,058	609	3,809	945
COTTON RAW						
Bel-Lux	159	$ 64	463	$ 335	89	$ 57
France			6,205	5,039	11,873	8,769
Germany	3,844	4,203	5,836	4,563	2,460	1,797
Italy	465	388	1,962	1,481	8,293	5,884
Netherlands	53	11	710	522		
CARPETS ETC.						
Bel-Lux	134	$ 486	141	$ 476	143	$ 531
France	139	912	197	1,123	144	971
Germany	191	1,141	771	3,663	1,145	7,259
Italy	195	293	169	334	188	225
Netherlands	18	69	19	78	26	139

Source: Same as Table 15.

TABLE 17

Major Iraqi exports (excluding petroleum) to the Common Market
(V in thousands of dollars; Q in metric tons)

Destination	1952 Q	1952 V	1954 Q	1954 V	1956 Q	1956 V
DRIED FRUITS						
Bel-Lux						
France						
Germany	3,621	$ 534				
Italy			263	$ 13		
Netherlands						
FRUIT NUTS FRESH						
Bel-Lux	276	$ 42	245	$ 31	413	$ 52
France						
Germany			4,882	692	7,321	776
Italy	2,661	175	6,138	337	5,424	304
Netherlands	319	57	203	27	100	18
BARLEY UNMILLED						
Bel-Lux	2,011	$ 163	46,879	$2,412	25,405	$1,575
France						
Germany	42,784	4,504	109,602	6,057	60,990	3,948
Italy			21,357	1,205	39,393	2,539
Netherlands	6,173	539	145,345	7,609	22,391	1,426

Source: Same as Table 15.

TABLE 18

Major Israeli exports to the Common Market
(V in thousands of dollars; Q in metric tons)

Destination	1952 Q	1952 V	1954 Q	1954 V	1956 Q	1956 V
		FRUIT	NUTS	FRESH		
Bel-Lux	5,283	$ 654	13,734	$1,532	11,286	$1,393
France			12,287	1,277	15,465	2,594
Germany			10,812	1,696	29,587	4,407
Italy					167	23
Netherlands	9,388	1,191	19,617	2,342	13,941	2,117
		OIL	SEEDS	ETC.		
Bel-Lux						
France			143	$ 53		
Germany					1,243	$ 481
Italy					327	119
Netherlands			163	58		

Source: Same as Table 15.

TABLE 19

Major Lebanese exports to the Common Market
(V in thousands of dollars; Q in metric tons)

Destination	1952		1954		1956	
	Q	V	Q	V	Q	V
FRUIT NUTS FRESH						
Bel-Lux					7	$ 11
France	2,910	$551			1,797	498
Germany	293	64	586	$ 149	255	33
Italy			56	10		
Netherlands						
VEGETABLES FRESH DRY						
Bel-Lux	121	$ 25	2,435	$ 181	1,080	$115
France			11,425	1,816	5,941	764
Germany	1,432	121	118	18	598	146
Italy						
Netherlands					112	16

Source: Same as Table 15.

TABLE 20

Major Syrian exports to the Common Market
(*V in thousands of dollars; Q in metric tons*)

Destination	1952 Q	1952 V	1954 Q	1954 V	1956 Q	1956 V
BARLEY UNMILLED						
Bel-Lux	2,778	$ 185	95,115	$ 4,830	61,349	$ 3,832
France						
Germany			89,537	5,339	79,317	5,113
Italy			720	39	2,588	167
Netherlands			84,957	4,377	16,140	982
WHEAT UNMILLED						
Bel-Lux			6,221	$ 507	430	$ 48
France					12,553	1,520
Germany	19,179	$ 2,145	100,732	10,028	19,515	2,053
Italy	9,699	905	12,338	1,152		
Netherlands			4,073	373		
COTTON						
Bel-Lux	207	$ 172	248	$ 163	895	$ 652
France	17,081	19,378	22,754	19,644	29,370	21,495
Germany	1,301	1,380	6,675	5,269	4,873	3,497
Italy	633	605	2,324	1,911	6,527	4,777
Netherlands						

Source: Same as Table 15.

TABLE 21

Major Turkish exports to the Common Market
(V in thousands of dollars; Q in metric tons)

Destination	1952 Q	1952 V	1954 Q	1954 V	1956 Q	1956 V
		FRUIT NUTS FRESH				
Bel-Lux	553	$ 418	227	$ 205	328	$ 391
France	464	393	1,274	1,192	1,919	2,338
Germany	13,959	8,782	12,193	10,850	13,093	15,292
Italy	742	526	119	79		
Netherlands	482	338	405	373	548	673
		DRIED FRUIT				
Bel-Lux	3,041	$ 844	4,099	$ 966	3,995	$ 1,203
France	2,460	748	3,654	973	4,449	1,403
Germany	15,748	4,093	8,045	1,733	5,456	1,438
Italy	3,500	982	8,686	1,358	4,559	1,402
Netherlands	4,944	1,334	6,516	1,429	6,160	1,849
		TOBACCO UNMANUFACTURED				
Bel-Lux	1,823	$ 1,349	1,975	$ 1,400	1,052	$ 848
France	2,504	1,763	2,616	2,540	1,500	2,122
Germany	5,906	6,135	6,793	7,822	7,251	9,736
Italy	952	702	658	1,180	1,127	2,183
Netherlands	1,056	846	3,471	4,419	2,908	4,394
		COTTON				
Bel-Lux	48	$ 33	100	$ 77	7,616	$ 6,259
France	16,799	17,613	7,730	6,482	5,352	3,802
Germany	27,824	30,330	11,118	8,956	15,114	12,558
Italy	6,531	6,365	12,964	11,067	414	337
Netherlands			24	18		
		CARPETS ETC.				
Bel-Lux	1	$ 16	3	$ 23	5	$ 21
France						
Germany	46	272	14	74	12	83
Italy	6	22	6	22		
Netherlands					4	22

Source: Same as Table 15.

TABLE 22

Major nonpetroleum exports of the Middle East to the Common Market in 1961

(in thousands of dollars)

Commodity	Egypt	Iran	Iraq	Israel	Lebanon	Syria	Turkey
Barley			$ 17				
Wheat				$ 580			$ 25
Rice	$ 2,319						
Vegetables	7,013	$ 393		120	$ 14	$ 645	3,967
Fruit nuts fresh	408	742	273	13,639	61	20	27,538
Dried fruits		5,913	309		88		13,784
Cotton	41,246	15,567		441	96	19,534	44,047
Tobacco		69			232	779	12,515
Carpets etc.	47	24,375	26		14		409

Source: Statistical Offices of the European Communities, *Foreign Trade Statistics*.

TABLE 23

Major exports of the Middle East (excluding petroleum [a]) to the United Kingdom

(V in thousands of dollars; Q in metric tons)

Country	Year	BARLEY Q	V	WHEAT Q	V	RICE Q	V	VEGETABLES DRY Q	V	FRUIT NUTS FRESH Q	V
Egypt	1952					1,206	$ 204	31,829	$3,324		
	1954					824	103	57,274	2,808		
	1956							53,421	4,462		
Iran	1952									189	$ 174
	1954									98	96
	1956										
Iraq	1952	192,742	$20,714								
	1954	46,663	2,621								
	1956	17,612	1,131								
Israel	1952									82,334	12,268
	1954									154,123	20,320
	1956									122,437	18,444
Lebanon	1952							3,759	136	324	43
	1954							1,518	121	119	40
	1956							3,709	351		

142

Syria	1952	113,417	11,614
	1954	450	28
	1956	505	33
		18,496	$ 1,732
Turkey	1952	2,530	2,199
	1954	4,770	4,388
	1956	2,741	3,249

		DRIED FRUIT b		COTTON b		TOBACCO UNMAN. b		RUGS ETC. b	
Egypt	1952			14,485	28,093				
	1954			35,001	37,225				
	1956			8,455	8,380				
Iran	1952	3,631	1,245	76	78			Not given	2,118
	1954	2,034	811	2,017	1,590				2,966
	1956	2,413	678	4,324	3,002				4,544
Iraq	1952	29,597	5,359						
	1954	6,427	1,056						
	1956	4,975	960						
Syria	1952			12,564	16,533				
	1954			6,064	4,911				
	1956			4,628	3,471				
Turkey	1952	17,478	4,653	1,251	1,611	258	259	Not given	21
	1954	19,787	4,808	150	115	1,288	1,940		
	1956	12,329	3,804	2,733	1,255	1,197	2,148		

Source: Same as Table 15.

[a] For exports of oil and petroleum products, see Tables 4–7.
[b] The source gives no data on these items for Israel and Lebanon for the years 1952, 1954, and 1956.

INDEX

Index

147

THE MIDDLE EAST AND THE EUROPEAN COMMON MARKET

was composed, printed, and bound
by Vail-Ballou Press, Inc.
for The University Press of Virginia.
The types used are Linotype Electra and Times Roman
with Monotype Times Roman display.
The paper is Warren's Old Style Antique
made by the S. D. Warren Company.
The book was designed by John J. Walklet, Jr.

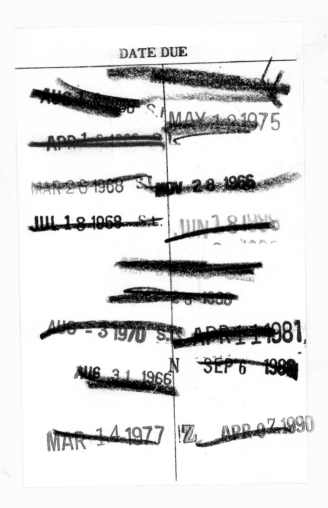

DATE DUE